D1398942

AMERICA'S
FORGOTTEN
FOUNDERS

EDITED BY

GARY L. GREGG II
AND MARK DAVID HALL

ISBN 978-1-884532-81-8

Book Design by Scott Stortz

Printed in USA

Published by
Butler Books
P.O. Box 7311
Louisville, KY 40207
(502) 897-9393
Fax (502) 897-9797

www.butlerbooks.com

Acknowledgments

As in any such endeavor, the editors have numerous people to whom we owe our gratitude. First, there are all those men and women, distinguished scholars all, who took the time to complete our survey and respond to our questions. Their names and brief biographies are found in the back of this volume. Unless otherwise noted, all quotes about the forgotten founders in this book come from these scholars.

We are particularly grateful to our colleagues who agreed to write chapters under an extremely tight deadline to help our readers learn more about the extraordinary accomplishments of those identified as our top ten greatest Founders who have been largely forgotten. To all of these men and women we owe a considerable debt.

The survey itself would not have been possible if it were not for the diligent and good work of a number of staff and students who aided in the project. Derek Jones, Malana Salyer, Neil Salyer, Maria Teresa dela Cruz, Mary Kate Lindsey, Christopher McCloskey, and Laura Hunzinger all deserve our appreciation.

Most significantly, we need to recognize the accomplishments of the forgotten Founders profiled in this volume, and the men and women who gave their lives, shed their blood, and toiled with their minds and pens to create the American Republic. We owe them much. The least we can do is remember, and we hope this project will help us pay that debt.

Gary L. Gregg II and Mark David Hall

Table of Contents

Introduction   1

James Wilson   11

George Mason   25

Gouverneur Morris   41

John Jay   53

Roger Sherman   67

John Marshall   79

John Dickinson   91

Thomas Paine   103

Patrick Henry   119

John Witherspoon   131

Conclusion   144

Appendix A: Contributors   151

Appendix B: Complete List of Nominated People   156

Appendix C: The Top Thirty Finalists   158

Appendix D: Participating Scholars   160

About the McConnell Center   176

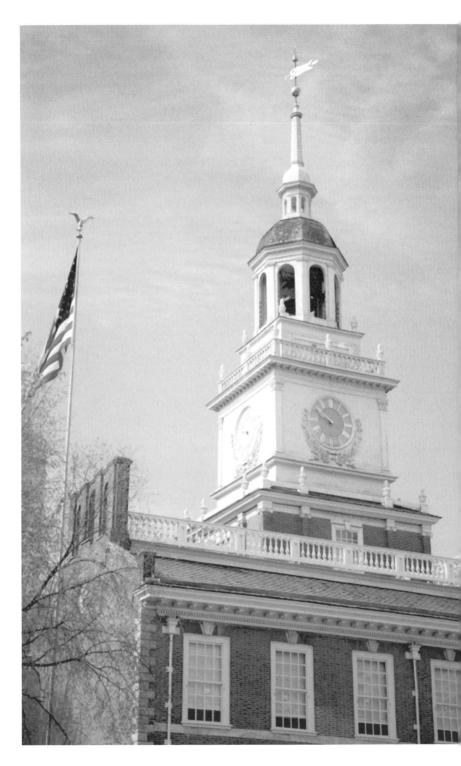

Introduction

When Americans think of the Founding Fathers, only a handful of leaders generally come to mind. Although the list may vary slightly from person to person, names like Benjamin Franklin, George Washington, John Adams, Thomas Jefferson, James Madison and Alexander Hamilton inevitably surface. In some respects this is not surprising given that by any measure these statesmen are among the most important and influential men in American history. A narrow focus on these great men, however, does not tell the full story of the American Founding experience and can be misleading in several ways:

(1) It is tempting to generalize from these six men to all of the Founders, but it is not self-evident that their views represent those held by all Founders. Indeed, our own research indicates that at least in some cases they do not.

(2) As with most history, the list is biased towards "winners." Some men and women on the losing side of important debates and actions – such as the declaration of American independence and ratification of the U.S. Constitution – made significant contributions to America's Founding.

(3) The list may be biased in terms of race and gender. Even acknowledging the cultural facts of the period, there is no denying that there were women and racial minorities who played significant, if largely unrecognized, roles in the overall events that

comprise the American Founding.

(4) The list favors men who served prominently in the executive branch of government. It is noteworthy that four of the six most readily recognizable Founders served as President of the United States of America.

American University's Daniel L. Dreisbach, in a wonderful essay entitled "Founders Famous and Forgotten," addresses the question of why some Founders are remembered and others are not. He argues that, in general, the famous Founders were recognized as great in their own day, came from power centers in the new nation, supported the Declaration of Independence and/or the new Constitution, left a voluminous paper trail, and (with the exception of Franklin) played prominent roles in the new national government. He does not suggest that the famous Founders were not great men, but he does contend that there is "a much larger company of statesmen who made salient contributions in thought, word, and deed to the construction of America's republican institutions." We agree.

In order to promote study of a wider range of Founders, we asked more than one hundred history, political science, and law professors who have written on the Founding Era to respond to the following question:

> Who are the Founders that have been neglected
> in American history texts and in public knowledge
> but who played significant enough roles to be
> remembered or whose example and thought
> should be remembered in America today?

For the purpose of the survey, we defined "Founders" as "the broad group of men and women who helped secure America's independence from Great Britain and/or helped establish the new constitutional republic and its political institutions." These individuals may or may not have held political office, and in some instances they may have even been on the "losing" side of history with respect to some issues.

Our respondents listed 73 men and women whom they believed have been unjustly neglected by history. The complete list is found in Appendix B at the back of this volume.

We were surprised and encouraged by the wide range of names suggested by our respondents. Their responses raise a number of questions, but none more intriguing than "who should count as a Founder?" For instance, should Founders include men and women such as:

Nancy Ward/Nanye-hi (c. 1738-1822), a female Cherokee leader who advocated peaceful co-existence with whites.

George Whitefield (1714-1770) the English minister whose preaching tours of America helped spark the First Great Awakening (1730s-1740s).

Phillis Wheatley (1753-1784) the African-American poet who was born into slavery.

John Marshall (1755-1834), the great Chief Justice whose primary contributions to the creation of the American Republic were made after 1800.

Ezra Stiles (1727-1795), the Congregationalist clergyman and president of Yale College who never held a political office.

The diversity reflected on the list of Founders produced by our survey points to the difficulty scholars have in untangling the extremely complex web of events and personalities that make up any human endeavor, particularly those from a distant past. Who can really account for the importance of the whispered word of advice on some late night after the children have gone off to bed or the chance meeting of men in an inn the night before a key decision would be made? Who can truly understand the ultimate impact of any one man or woman and how history might have been different if they had not lived or engaged in the world of affairs? We appreciate the efforts of our survey participants to untangle some of history's webs.

Without discounting the value of considering a wide range of individuals, for the purposes of this survey we wanted to see if scholars could agree on a short list of important but neglected Founders. Accordingly, we submitted the names of the thirty Founders who were mentioned most often in the first round of our survey to the original group of academics. We asked these historians, political scientists and law professors to rank the top ten Founders in this group in order of importance. In making this request we acknowledged that "'importance' is not easily quantifiable," but stipulated that "we are interested to see if a general consensus emerges as to the top tier of forgotten Founders."

The respondents ranked Founders on a scale of 1-10, with one being the most important. We weighted each vote, assigning ten points for a first place vote, nine for a second place vote, etc. We then calculated the number of points received by each forgotten Founder. The Pennsylvania Scot James Wilson received the most points by a significant margin, making us wonder why he is not better known among the general public. Indeed, he outpolled arguably better-known men like George Mason, Patrick Henry, and Thomas Paine by huge margins.

The consensus top ten Founders, according to our survey, are:

Rank	Founder	Points
1	James Wilson	214
2	George Mason	152
3	Gouverneur Morris	128
4	John Jay	125
5	Roger Sherman	124
6	John Marshall	117
7	John Dickinson	92
8	Thomas Paine	76
9	Patrick Henry	71
10	John Witherspoon	68

After Witherspoon, the total number of points for each Founder begins to drop precipitously. For instance, the lowest ten vote recipients received a total of 103 points, fewer points than any of the first six forgotten Founders received by themselves. The complete list of thirty finalists and their point totals may be found in Appendix C.

Before we proceed, two caveats are in order. First, we would like to emphasize that we are not arguing that we have "scientifically" determined a list of Founders who deserve to be added to the pantheon of famous elites. We do think, however, it is interesting that there is a clear consensus among experts on the era about a relatively short list of significant but neglected Founders. By any measure, each of the ten men on our list played important roles in either the Revolution or the creation of the American Republic, and five of them were significantly involved in both.

Second, we recognize that one might object that John Marshall is neither "forgotten" nor a "Founder." Certainly he is reasonably well known–although not nearly as famous as the six most recognizable Founders. More significant is the complaint that he should not be considered a Founder because his primary contributions were made after 1800. Although he served in the Revolution and the Virginia ratifying convention, if he had died in 1800 there is no chance he would be on our list of forgotten Founders. Nevertheless, because we defined Founders as "the broad group of men and women who helped . . . establish the new constitutional republic and its political institutions," it is reasonable to view him as playing a critical role in this enterprise.

It is noteworthy that none of our top ten forgotten Founders played a significant role in the executive branch of the national government (although Marshall served as Secretary of State for almost a year and Morris was Minister Plenipotentiary to France from 1792-1794). Sherman and Marshall served briefly in the

House of Representatives, and Sherman and Morris were United States Senators. As well, Wilson, Jay, and Marshall served on the Supreme Court, but only Marshall can lay claim to making a significant impact from the bench. With the exception of Marshall, none of these men played a "prominent" role in the new national government. Indeed, five of our forgotten Founders died before 1800. Thus, there is a striking difference between our list here and that of the most recognizable six figures. It says something about how the establishment of the new government after 1787 is treated in our history books compared to the period of preparation immediately preceding it.

Each of the top ten forgotten Founders was reasonably well known in the Founding Era, and most of them were well regarded for their mastery of the written or spoken word. However, none left an extensive collection of papers. The papers of Marshall, Paine, and Witherspoon have been published in twelve, ten, and nine volumes, respectively. Otherwise, papers of these forgotten Founders have been published in collections ranging between one and four volumes–if they have been published at all. By contrast, George Washington's papers are projected to fill 90 volumes, the Adams family papers 100, Jefferson's will run approximately 75, and James Madison and Benjamin Franklin papers projects are expected to contain at least 50 volumes.

Each of our top forgotten Founders was on the "winning side" of history with three minor exceptions. John Dickinson famously refused to vote for the Declaration of Independence, but supported the War for Independence in a variety of other ways, and he later helped draft and supported the U.S. Constitution. George Mason and Patrick Henry, on the other hand, were ardent supporters of the Revolution, but each opposed the adoption of the Constitution.

It is striking that three of our top forgotten Founders—James Wilson, John Witherspoon, and Thomas Paine were recent immigrants, as was one of the most famous Founders—Alexander Hamilton. Moreover, each of these men, as well as Roger Sherman, John Marshall, and the famous Founder Benjamin Franklin, were from humble backgrounds. None of these individuals was born into abject poverty, but neither did they come from wealthy, established families. Unlike the Old World, America provided room for a variety of bright, hard-working (white) men to become important civic leaders.

Many readers of this work are undoubtedly familiar with most of the names on our list of forgotten Founders, but even specialists in the Founding era may not be able to explain why each of these individuals is significant. Accordingly, we have commissioned profiles of our top ten forgotten Founders. We hope these profiles encourage study and discussion of a wide range of Founders, but we do not think that the expanded discussion should be limited to them. Following these profiles we offer a brief discussion of America's other forgotten Founders.

"The pyramid of government–and a republican government may well receive that beautiful and solid form–should be raised to a dignified altitude: but its foundations must, of consequence, be broad and strong, and deep. The authority, the interests, and the affections of the people at large are the only foundation, on which a superstructure, proposed to be at once durable and magnificent, can be rationally erected."

–James Wilson, *Lectures on Law,* 1791.

"Without liberty, law loses its nature and its name, and becomes oppression. Without law, liberty also loses its nature and its name, and becomes licentiousness."

–James Wilson, *Lectures on Law,* 1791.

James Wilson
(1742-1798)

MARK DAVID HALL

James Wilson was a "reluctant revolutionary," but he played a significant role in the American Revolution and was a signer of the Declaration of Independence. He was one of the most important delegates at the Federal Constitutional Convention, where he argued consistently for a strong and democratic national government. His early defense of the proposed Constitution and his leadership in the Pennsylvania ratifying convention did much to secure the Constitution's approval. Wilson served as one of the new nation's first Supreme Court Justices, and his Lectures on Law *contain some of the period's most profound commentary of the Constitution and American law.*

Wilson was born in Carskerdo, Scotland in 1742, the son of a lower-middle-class farmer. Dedicated to the ministry at birth, he received a solid classical education that enabled him to win a scholarship to the University of St. Andrews. Wilson studied there for four years before entering the university's divinity school, St. Mary's, in 1761. He was forced to withdraw in 1762 upon the death of his father, and for a few years served as a tutor to support his family. The life of a pedagogue did not suit Wilson, so as soon as his siblings were old enough to support their mother he immigrated to America in search of greater opportunities. Arriving in Pennsylvania in 1765, Wilson taught Latin and Greek at the College of Philadelphia for a year before reading law under John Dickinson. He flourished as an attorney, and as the Revolution approached, was drawn into politics.

Historian Christopher Collier proposed that Wilson was a "polemicist the equal of Tom Paine." This may be an exaggeration, but it is indisputable that Wilson achieved national recognition with his essay, "Considerations on the Nature and Extent of the Legislative Authority of the British Parliament" (1774). Many Patriots rejected Parliament's claim that it could levy internal taxes on the colonies, but they conceded that it could regulate and/or tax international trade. Wilson's essay was the first to publicly deny the "legislative authority of the British Parliament over the colonies . . . *in every instant.*" He acknowledged that the colonists owed allegiance to the King in exchange for his protection, but stipulated that if he withdrew his protection the colonists were no longer obligated to obey the Crown. Wilson was able to put this theory into practice after he was appointed to the Second Continental Congress. He was, in Terence Ball's words, "a reluctant revolutionary," but he actively participated in the proceedings and eventually cast a critical vote in favor of independence.

> "Revolutionary tract writer, member of Constitutional Congress, prominent member of Constitutional Convention, and federalist, Supreme Court justice, legal theorist."
>
> —Ralph Ketcham

By the late 1770s Wilson was recognized as one of the finest attorneys in America. In 1779, he was appointed to be France's advocate-general in the United States. He served in this position until

1783 when he resigned because King Louis XVI was unwilling to pay the high fees he required (the king eventually paid him 10,000 livres for his services). In 1782, Pennsylvania asked Wilson to represent the state in a land dispute with Connecticut. The case was argued before a tribunal formed under Article IX of the Articles of Confederation, and Wilson's careful arguments won the day. His legal prominence is illustrated as well by General Washington's willingness to pay him one hundred guineas to accept his nephew, Bushrod, as a law student. Bushrod, aware that such a fee was well above the going rate, begged his uncle to allow him to study elsewhere. But Washington was convinced of Wilson's ability as a lawyer and insisted on him, although he had to pay the fee with a promissory note. Bushrod was evidently well served by this arrangement, as indicated by his successful legal career and eventual appointment to his mentor's seat on the Supreme Court of the United States.

In his 1785 pamphlet, "Considerations on the Bank of North America," Wilson made the provocative argument that even under the Articles of Confederation, "[t]o many purposes, the United States are to be considered as one undivided, independent nation." Moreover, he proposed that Congress possessed a variety of implied powers, including the power to charter a national bank, and he vigorously defended the necessity of such a bank. Numerous scholars have noted that the essay contains every argument later made by Alexander Hamilton and his allies in support of a national bank under the United States Constitution.

In 1787 the Pennsylvania legislature appointed Wilson to represent the state at the Constitutional Convention. He attended the Convention from start to finish, and he participated in all of the most significant proceedings. Wilson joined with Madison to argue for a powerful national government based immediately upon the authority of the people. He was the most democratic of all delegates, arguing for the direct, popular, and proportional election of Representatives, Senators, and the President. When his colleagues rejected the direct election of the President–George Mason said "it would be as unnatural to refer the choice of the proper character for chief Magistrate to the people, as it would, to refer a trial of colours to a blind man"–Wilson, according to Carol Berkin, "devised the electoral college" or, in Collier's words, he became the "father of the bastard electoral college."

> "Mr. Wilson ranks among the foremost in legal and political knowledge. . . No man is more clear, copious, and comprehensive than Mr. Wilson, yet he is no great Orator. He draws attention not by the charm of his eloquence, but by the force of his reasoning."
>
> —William Pierce, Wilson's colleague at the Federal Convention of 1787

Wilson believed that the chief executive should be independent of the legislature, and that he should have a range of powers that would allow him to act with "vigor and dispatch." As well, he fought for an independent federal judiciary that would possess the power of judicial review. Indeed, throughout the Convention he was one of the most significant advocates of checks and balances and the separation of powers. Wilson had more faith in the people than most Founders, but he was convinced that concentrated power, even power concentrated in a legislature, would lead to disaster. In his *Lectures on Law*, he wrote that a "single legislature is calculated to unite in it all the pernicious qualities of the different extremes of bad government." Finally, it is important to note that Wilson served on the critical five-member Committee of Detail, and many of the earliest full drafts of the Constitution are in his handwriting.

Under Wilson's leadership, Pennsylvania became the second state, and the first large one, to ratify the Constitution. As the only member of the state's ratifying convention who attended the Federal Convention, Wilson was in an excellent position to defend the Constitution. In his "State House Yard Speech" of October 6, 1787, he responded to the earliest Anti-Federalist criticisms. Gordon Wood, in *The Creation of the American Republic*, remarked that this speech quickly became "the basis of all Federalist thinking." Wilson did his job so well that Federalists throughout the country enlisted his aid in their states' ratification debates. George Washington, for instance, sent a copy of the speech to a friend, noting:

> [T]he enclosed *Advertiser* contains a speech of Mr. Wilson's, as able, candid, and honest member as was in the convention, which will place most of Colonel Mason's objections in their true point of light, I send it to you. The republication of it, if you can get it done, will be serviceable at this juncture.

By the end of 1787, the speech had been reprinted in thirty-four newspapers in twelve states, and it was circulated in pamphlet form throughout the nation. Bernard Bailyn wrote in *The Ideological Origins of the American Revolution* that "in the 'transient circumstances' of the time it was not so much the *Federalist* papers that captured most people's imaginations as James Wilson's speech of October 6, 1787, the most famous, to some the most notorious, federalist statement of the time." Similarly, political scientist Gordon Lloyd commented that the "State-House speech is vital for an understanding of the pamphlet exchanges during the struggle for ratification." Following the ratification of the U.S. Constitution, Wilson played a major role in the Pennsylvania constitutional convention of 1789-90.

"James Wilson was arguably the best legal theorist of the Founders . . ."

–Garry Wills

George Washington appointed Wilson to be Associate Justice of the United States Supreme Court in 1789. The Court had relatively little business during its first decade, but Wilson issued significant opinions or votes in several cases, including *Hylton v. U.S.* (1796), *Ware v. Hylton* (1796), and *Chisholm v. Georgia* (1793). Particularly important is his seriatim opinion in *Chisholm*. In this case the Court had to determine if Alexander Chisholm, a citizen of South Carolina, could sue the state of Georgia. Georgia claimed he could not because it was a sovereign state. Wilson famously responded that "[a]s to the purposes of the Union . . . Georgia is NOT a sovereign State." He reasoned that by ratifying the Constitution, the citizens of Georgia gave the federal judiciary, in the language of Article III, the power to judge controversies "between a State and Citizens of another State." This ruling provoked an immediate storm of outrage. There was talk of impeachment, and the day after the decision an amendment was introduced in Congress to overturn it. With the ratification of the

Eleventh Amendment in 1795 the Court's decision in *Chisholm* was negated, but Wilson's opinion remains an important statement of the basic principles of American federalism.

Perhaps the most significant but overlooked case with which Wilson was involved concerned The Invalid Pension Act of 1792. The law required federal judges to act as administrators to determine whether veterans were eligible for certain benefits. In *Hayburn's Case* (1792), Wilson, who was riding circuit, led Justice John Blair and District Court Judge Richard Peters to declare the act unconstitutional because it required judges to perform non-judicial duties. Congress rapidly altered the act to meet Wilson's objections, so the Supreme Court never heard the case. Accordingly, *Hayburn's Case* is often overlooked as the first instance where a federal court declared an act of Congress to be unconstitutional.

From 1790 to 1792, Wilson offered a series of law lectures at the College of Philadelphia–today the University of Pennsylvania. Because he believed that law should be "studied and practised as a science founded in principle" not "followed as a trade depending merely upon precedent," many of his lectures are devoted to broad moral, epistemological, political, and jurisprudential issues. Consequently, they contain some of the richest analysis of America's constitutional order written by a Founder. Their significance was recognized by many survey participants. For instance, Garry Wills suggested that "Wilson was arguably the best legal theorist of the Founders." In a similar vein, Howard Lubert called Wilson "a leading legal authority of the age," and Walter Nicgorski wrote that he was "a ranging, profound, and bold thinker, both about the principles of good government and about specific constitutional devices," while Henry J. Abraham referred to him as "one of the outstanding lawyer scholars of his time."

> "Wilson was second to James Madison in importance in framing the Constitution. Wilson was also the leading American legal theorist of his day. "
>
> —Scott Gerber

In the early 1770s Wilson began speculating heavily in western land. In 1797 an economic downturn devastated an over-leveraged Wilson. Even though he was a sitting Supreme Court Justice, he was thrown into jail on two separate occasions because of unpaid debts. He spent his final days hiding from creditors in Edenton, North Carolina. Wilson died on August 21, 1798, and was buried with little ceremony in Edenton. In 1906 his body was disinterred and reburied in America's Westminster Abbey–Christ Church, Philadelphia.

Wilson's inglorious and early death, his lack of papers, and his service on the Supreme Court at a time when there was little business before that body, conspired to keep him in relative obscurity. However, he is worthy of serious consideration as one of the most thoughtful and systematic political and legal theorists of the Founding Era. He played a critical role at the Constitutional Convention, and although he did not win every battle, the American constitutional system has developed over time to closely resemble his vision. In his law lectures, Wilson wrote that:

> There is not in the whole science of politicks a more solid or a more important maxim than this–that of all governments, those are the best, which, by the natural effect of their constitutions, are frequently drawn back to their first principles.

If American citizens, like governments, should reflect upon the first principles of our constitutional republic, the political and legal ideas of one of the greatest theorists among the Founders simply cannot be ignored.

MAIN CONTRIBUTIONS OF JAMES WILSON

Wilson played a critical role in drafting the United States Constitution. He consistently argued for a strong and democratic national government that would protect the natural rights of its citizens.

Wilson offered one of the earliest and most influential responses to Anti-Federalist criticisms of the Constitution. Under his leadership, Pennsylvania became the second state to ratify the document.

Wilson was one of the leading political and legal theorists among all of the Founders.

From the Pen of James Wilson

"Of law there are different kinds. All, however, may be arranged in two different classes. 1. Divine. 2. Human laws. The descriptive epithets employed denote, that the former have God, the latter, man, for their author. The laws of God may be divided into the following species.

I. That law, the book of which we are neither able nor worthy to open. Of this law, the author and observer is God. He is a law to himself, as well as to all created things. This law we may name the "law eternal."

II. That law, which is made for angels and the spirits of the just made perfect. This may be called the "law celestial." This law, and the glorious state for which it is adapted, we see, at present, but darkly and as through a glass: but hereafter we shall see even as we are seen; and shall know even as we are known. From the wisdom and the goodness of the adorable Author and Preserver of the universe, we are justified in concluding, that the celestial and perfect state is governed, as all other things are, by his established laws. What those laws are, it is not yet given us to know; but on one truth we may rely with sure and certain confidence – those laws are wise and good. For another truth we have infallible authority – those laws are strictly obeyed: "In heaven his will is done."

III. That law, by which the irrational and inanimate parts of the creation are governed. The great Creator of all things has established general and fixed rules, according to which all the phenomena of the material universe are produced and regulated. These rules are usually denominated laws of nature. The science, which has those laws for its object, is distinguished by the name of natural philosophy. It is sometimes called, the philosophy of body. Of this science, there are numerous branches.

IV. That law, which God has made for man in his present state; that law, which is communicated to us by reason and conscience, the divine monitors within us, and by the sacred oracles, the divine monitors without us. This law has undergone several subdivisions, and has been known by distinct appellations, according to the different ways in which it has been promulgated, and the different objects which it respects.

As promulgated by reason and the moral sense, it has been called natural; as promulgated by the holy scriptures, it has been called revealed law.

As addressed to men, it has been denominated the law of nature; as addressed to political societies, it has been denominated the law of nations.

But it should always be remembered, that this law, natural or revealed, made for men or for nations, flows from the same divine source: it is the law of God.

Nature, or, to speak more properly, the Author of nature, has done much for us; but it is his gracious appointment and will, that we should also do much for ourselves. What we do, indeed, must be founded on what he has done; and the deficiencies of our laws must be supplied by the perfections of his. Human law must rest its authority, ultimately, upon the authority of that law, which is divine.

Of that law, the following are maxims – that no injury should be done – that a lawful engagement, voluntarily made, should be faithfully fulfilled. We now see the deep and the solid foundations of human law.

It is of two species. 1. That which a political society makes for itself. This is municipal law. 2. That which two or more political societies make for themselves. This is the voluntary law of nations.

In all these species of law – the law eternal – the law celestial – the law natural – the divine law, as it respects men and nations – the human law, as it also respects men and nations – man is deeply and intimately concerned. Of all these species of law, therefore, the knowledge must be most important to man.

Those parts of natural philosophy, which more immediately relate to the human body, are appropriated to the profession of physick.

The law eternal, the law celestial, and the law divine, as they are disclosed by that revelation, which has brought life and immortality to light, are the more peculiar objects of the profession of divinity.

The law of nature, the law of nations, and the municipal law form the objects of the profession of law.

From this short, but plain and, I hope, just statement of things, we perceive a principle of connexion between all the learned professions; but especially between the two last mentioned. Far from being rivals or enemies, religion and law are twin sisters, friends, and mutual assistants. Indeed, these two sciences run into each other. The divine law, as discovered by reason and the moral sense, forms an essential part of both.

From this statement of things, we also perceive how important and dignified the profession of the law is, when traced to its sources, and viewed in its just extent.

The immediate objects of our attention are, the law of nature, the law of nations, and the municipal law. On the two first of these three great heads, I shall be very general. On the last, especially on those parts of it, which comprehend the constitutions and publick law, I shall be more particular and minute."

–James Wilson, *Lectures on Law* (1791)

RECOMMENDED READING

Kermit L. Hall and Mark David Hall, ed. *Collected Works of James Wilson*, 2 vols. (Indianapolis: Liberty Fund Press, 2007).

Charles Page Smith, *James Wilson: Founding Father, 1742-1798* (Chapel Hill: University of North Carolina Press, 1956).

Mark David Hall, *The Political and Legal Philosophy of James Wilson,1742-1798* (Columbia: The University of Missouri Press, 1997).

"Every Member of Society is in Duty bound to contribute to the Safety & Good of the Whole; and when the Subject is of such Importance as the Liberty & Happiness of a Country, every inferior Consideration, as well as the Inconvenience to a few Individuals, must give place to it; nor is this any Hardship upon them; as themselves & their Posterity are to partake of the Benefits resulting from it."

–George Mason to Richard Henry Lee, June 7, 1770.

"We came equals into this world, and equals shall we go out of it. All men are by nature born equally free and independent. To protect the weaker from the injuries and insults of the stronger were societies first formed. . . . Every society, all government, and every kind of civil compact therefore, is or ought to be, calculated for the general good and safety of the community. Every power, every authority vested in particular men is, or ought to be, ultimately directed to this sole end; and whenever any power or authority whatever extends further, or is of longer duration than is in its nature necessary for these purposes, it may be called government, but it is in fact oppression. . . . In all our associations; in all our agreements let us never lose sight of this fundamental maxim – that all power was originally lodged in, and consequently is derived from, the people. We should wear it as a breastplate, and buckle it on as our armour."

–George Mason, Remarks on Annual Election for the
Fairfax Independent Company, April 1775.

"Slavery discourages arts & manufactures. The poor despise labor when performed by slaves. They prevent the immigration of Whites, who really enrich & strengthen a Country. They produce the most pernicious effect on manners. Every master of slaves is born a petty tyrant. They bring the judgment of heaven on a Country. As nations can not be rewarded or punished in the next world they must be in this. By an inevitable chain of causes & effects providence punishes national sins, by national calamities."

–George Mason, Speech in Constitutional Convention,
August 22, 1787.

GEORGE MASON
(1725-1792)

DANIEL L. DREISBACH

George Mason played pivotal roles in important representative assemblies of his state and nation, including Virginia Conventions in 1775 and 1776, the Constitutional Convention of 1787, and the Virginia ratifying convention in June 1788. His contributions to the political documents of the Founding era are his most enduring legacy. He was the principal draftsman of the Fairfax Resolves, Virginia's first state constitution, and, most famously, Virginia's Declaration of Rights, which is still enshrined in the Commonwealth's laws. The Virginia Declaration influenced numerous state, national, and international declarations of rights and informed essential phrases in the U.S. Declaration of Independence. At the Constitutional Convention of 1787, Mason labored to shape the national constitution, but, in the end, he refused to sign it and led the campaign to thwart its ratification. After unsuccessfully moving to add a bill of rights to the proposed national constitution, he became a leading advocate for such a bill, which was eventually added to the U.S. Constitution in December 1791.

George Mason IV (1725-1792) was born on his family's Fairfax County plantation in December 1725. He inherited the estate a decade later when his father drowned in a boating accident on the Potomac River. The young Mason received little formal education, although he was tutored at home and read extensively in his uncle's library, one of the best in colonial Virginia. He married Ann Eilbeck of Maryland in 1750 – a marriage that, before Ann's death in 1773, produced twelve children, nine of whom survived to adulthood. During the marriage, Mason built a home he called Gunston Hall near the Potomac, a few miles south of Mount Vernon. He remarried in 1780 to Sarah Brent from a prominent Maryland family.

In addition to managing a prosperous plantation, Mason assumed a variety of community offices and responsibilities, including vestryman and church warden of Truro Parish, justice of the Fairfax County court, trustee of the city of Alexandria, and elected member of the House of Burgesses, the Commonwealth's colonial legislature. In the late 1740s, Mason invested in and later became an officer of the Ohio Company, which speculated in western lands. Representing the Company's disputed claims was a preoccupation of his adult life.

> "Author of the Virginia Bill of Rights who should be better known as the father of all bills of rights, especially the U.S. one of 1791. Also for his antislavery efforts in the Convention of 1787."
> —Christopher Collier

Starting in the mid-1760s, Mason began to articulate the colonists' claims to liberty and privileges as Englishmen and their grievances against the crown, especially onerous taxes. He drafted the Fairfax Resolves in July 1774, an influential statement expressing the colonists' constitutional rights and objections to British policies in the wake of the Boston Port Act. He also served on the Fairfax County Committee of Safety and the Committee of Correspondence. He was elected to represent Fairfax County at the Virginia Convention where he was the lead draftsman of the Virginia Declaration of Rights and Constitution of 1776.

He attended the Mount Vernon Conference in March 1785, an important prelude to the Annapolis Convention (to which Mason was an appointed delegate, but he did not attend) the following year and the Constitutional Convention that met in Philadelphia in 1787. Mason was appointed a Virginia representative to the Constitutional Convention. He was one of the most vocal delegates, contributing significantly to the course of debates and the shape of the final document. He failed, however, to carry the Convention on several issues of importance to him and, therefore, declined to sign the proposed constitution. He returned home and, in the final political campaign of his career, led the losing effort to defeat the Constitution in the Virginia ratifying convention held in Richmond in June 1788. Mason declined an appointment to the U.S. Senate under the new national Constitution and died at Gunston Hall, where he was buried in October 1792.

Today, Mason is best known as the principal draftsman of the Virginia Declaration of Rights, adopted on June 12, 1776. He was a Fairfax County delegate to the Virginia Convention, filling the seat vacated by George Washington, who had been appointed commander-in-chief of a continental army. The Convention of 1776, arguably the most noteworthy political body ever assembled in the Commonwealth's history, convened in Williamsburg on May 6, 1776. On May 15, the Convention passed a resolution instructing the Commonwealth's delegates at the Continental Congress to press for a declaration of independence from England. This bold initiative raised questions about the nature of civil authority extant in the Commonwealth. Believing, perhaps, that they had reverted to a state of nature, the delegates thought it necessary to frame a new social compact, beginning with a declaration of man's natural rights, followed by a new plan of civil government. The assembly appointed a committee to prepare a state declaration of rights and constitution. Among those appointed to the committee were Mason and the young, untested delegate from Orange County, James Madison, Jr.

Mason, whose considerable talents were well known in the Commonwealth, was a driving force in the Convention. Edmund Pendleton informed Thomas Jefferson that "Colo[nel] Mason seems to have the Ascendancy in the great work" of forming a new government in Virginia. Some time in late May, Mason prepared ten proposals for a declaration of rights to which other proposals were added by the committee. Committee drafts of the Declaration were printed and circulated widely up and down the Atlantic seaboard in late May and early June, and they had an immediate and profound impact on compatriots in the nascent states engaged in the task of creating new governments. Interestingly, a committee draft, not the version ultimately enacted, had the most influence in the other states.

The Virginia Declaration was printed in draft form, thoroughly debated, and amended before it was passed unanimously on June 12. The genius of Mason's Declaration of Rights was not that it expressed original principles; rather, it distilled and harmonized the republican sentiments of the day, brilliantly summarizing the objectives of those Americans who aspired to be independent and free. With remarkable brevity and clarity, it condensed the great principles of political freedom inherited from the British, including principles extracted from the Magna Carta, the Petition of Right, the English Bill of Rights, and the long struggle to establish parliamentary supremacy culminating in the Glorious Revolution of 1688. It combined a commitment to fundamental liberties with a brief expression of constitutional doctrines and political ideas expounded by Locke, Montesquieu, and other liberal political philosophers.

> "Nobody understood better (except maybe some Massachusetts townsmen) the meaning of popular sovereignty. He cared about rights. He deserves to be remembered with honor."
>
> —Pauline Maier

The Declaration of Rights, which Mason boasted was the "first in America," is acclaimed as a guidepost to the republican principles of the American Founding. By the end of the Founding era, every state had either framed a bill of rights or enacted legislation with similar provisions. Many states, including Pennsylvania, Maryland, North Carolina, Vermont, Delaware, New Hampshire, and Massachusetts, apparently undertook this task with a copy of the Virginia Declaration before them. The national Bill of Rights, ratified in 1791, similarly bears the unmistakable influence of Mason's Declaration. Christopher Collier, a scholar of the American Founding, said Mason "should be better known as the father of all bills of rights, especially the U.S. one of 1791."

The Declaration contains sixteen articles, affirming the "inherent rights" of life, liberty, property, and the pursuit of happiness and safety; describing government power as vested in and derived from the people; outlining the separation of the state's "legislative and executive powers" from the "judiciary;" and enumerating individual rights that are free from government restrictions. The first article famously declares (in a sentence that informed the opening lines of the U.S.

Declaration of Independence) "THAT all men are by nature equally free and independent, and have certain inherent rights . . . [that they cannot divest]; namely, the enjoyment of life and liberty, with the means of acquiring and possessing property, and pursuing and obtaining happiness and safety." Pauline Maier, an eminent historian of the Declaration of Independence, observed: Mason's "phrase 'all men are born equally free and independent' [as the phrase appeared in Mason's original draft] influenced the Declaration of Independence and one state's Declaration of Rights after another. Those are perhaps some of the most important words in any American Founding document."

Among the enumerated rights it sets forth are those of a criminal defendant to be informed of accusations, "confronted with the accusers and witnesses, to call for evidence in his favour, and to a speedy trial by an impartial jury of his vicinage"; the privilege against self-incrimination; the guarantee of due process of law; prohibitions on "excessive bail," "excessive fines," "cruel and unusual punishments," and unreasonable searches and seizures; the "freedom of the press"; and the "free exercise of religion."

After adopting the Declaration, the Convention turned its attention to framing a constitution or form of government. Once again, Mason was the chief architect. The Virginia Constitution of June 1776 was one of the first written state constitutions and a model followed by other states. Republican in character, the brief document separated the powers of the "legislative, executive, and judiciary departments," created a bicameral legislature whose members were elected by the people, placed term limits on key government offices, provided that government officials could be impeached for "mal-administration [or] corruption," and directed the legislature to elect the governor and appoint judges. One significant defect was that it failed to provide for an amending process. The constitution reflected the view, expressed in the Declaration of Rights, that the people are the source of all legitimate governmental power.

In December 1786, Virginia appointed Mason as one of its delegates to an assembly convened in Philadelphia to revise the Articles of Confederation. He agreed to serve. At the Constitutional Convention, he spoke more frequently than all but four delegates. His contributions confirmed that he was an astute student of law, politics, and constitutionalism.

He advocated popular elections, liberal suffrage requirements, the initiation of money bills in the House of Representatives, a three-person executive, a limited role for the federal judiciary, the admission of and full equality for new states in the west, and a termination of the importation of slaves. Although he depended on and profited from slave labor and declined in his lifetime or in his will to free his own slaves, he made several statements in the Convention against the peculiar institution and, more specifically, slave importation. "Slavery discourages arts & manufactures," he said in one speech. "They produce the most pernicious effect on manners. Every master of slaves is born a petty tyrant. They bring the judgment of heaven on a Country." Most famously, he championed a national declaration of rights. In the Convention's closing days, he spearheaded an effort to draw up a bill of rights. The state delegations unanimously rejected this initiative. The absence of support for Mason's proposal did not indicate hostility to the concept of rights. Rather, there was a consensus that the national government under the proposed constitution had no jurisdiction in matters pertaining to civil and religious liberties; and where no power had been granted, there was no need to check the abuse of power.

When the Convention failed to address his objections to the emerging national charter, especially the absence of a declaration of rights and the power given Congress to enact navigation laws by a simple majority vote, Mason exclaimed "that he would sooner chop off his right hand than put it to the Constitution as it now stands." Much to the consternation of the Constitution's supporters, Mason refused to sign the document. "Col. Mason left Philad[elphi]a in an exceeding ill humour indeed," James Madison reported. "He considers the want of a Bill of Rights as a fatal objection."

Before departing from Philadelphia in September 1787, Mason drafted a statement outlining his objections to the proposed national constitution. It was published shortly thereafter and widely circulated, framing the debate over the Constitution's ratification. As an incisive critic and active opponent of the proposed constitution, Mason (along with other articulate Anti-Federalists) defined and drove the debate on certain constitutional issues and features, especially the need for a national bill of rights. Many of the trenchant defenses of the Constitution were direct responses to Anti-Federalist critiques, such as Mason's.

"His thinking about rights is important to engage."

– Walter Nicgorski

Back in Virginia, Mason was elected to the state's ratifying convention where, in concert with Patrick Henry and William Grayson, he led the opposition to the proposed constitution. "No Bill of Rights" became the rallying slogan of Mason and the Anti-Federalists. The campaign in Virginia to derail ratification lost narrowly.

While the First Federal Congress was still debating amendments, Mason wrote: "I have received much Satisfaction from the Amendments to the federal Constitution, which have lately passed the House of Representatives; I hope they will also pass the Senate. With two or three further Amendments . . . I cou'd chearfully put my Hand & Heart to the new Government." The amendments Mason had in mind were so substantial and sweeping that the measures actually adopted almost certainly did not assuage his concerns. Nonetheless, he obtained a measure of satisfaction with the ratification of the national Bill of Rights in December 1791.

What explains Mason's relative obscurity today? The irascible, independent-minded Mason was a most reluctant public figure. He eschewed the spotlight, preferring to attend to the pressing demands of his family and plantation. He lacked the diplomatic skills, penchant for self-promotion, or gifts of soaring oratory that might have brought him more acclaim. His precarious health (a chronic affliction with gout for most of his adult life substantially interfered with public duties), truculent temperament, and aversion to political life all contributed to a diminished profile in the history of the Founding era. He declined an office in the national government under the ratified Constitution (refusing an appointment to the U.S. Senate) and died in 1792 at a time when more famous Founders were assuming leading roles on the newly available national stage. His outspoken opposition to the Constitution, more than anything, diminished his reputation as a Founder. Moreover, unlike the famous Founders, he died leaving relatively few papers and no memoirs documenting his salient contributions to his state and nation.

Although Mason is an almost forgotten Founder, he was recognized by his contemporaries as, in the words of Thomas Jefferson, "one of our really great men, and of the first order of greatness." In his *Autobiography*, Jefferson described Mason as a formidable debater, "one most steadfast, able and zealous. . . . This was George Mason, a man of the first order of wisdom among those who acted on the theatre of the revolution, of expansive mind, profound judgment, cogent in argument, learned in the lore of our former constitution, and earnest for the republican change on democratic principles." William Pierce, a Georgia delegate at the Constitutional Convention, said Mason was "a Gentleman of remarkable strong powers, and possesses a clear and copious understanding. He is able and convincing in debate, steady and firm in his principles, and undoubtedly one of the best politicians in America." James Madison thought that Mason possessed "the high character of a powerful Reasoner, a profound Statesman and a devoted Republican."

Significantly, Mason's contemporaries lamented that he had not been accorded the recognition and honor due to him. Philip Mazzei, the Italian physician, merchant, and admirer of American liberty, remarked: "in my opinion . . . he is not well enough known. He is one of those brave, rare-talented men who cause Nature a great effort to produce, – a Dante, a Macchiavelli, a Galileo, a Newton, a Franklin, a Turgot, an Elvezio, and so on." Madison opined, "It is to be regretted that highly distinguished as he was the memorials of them we record, or perhaps otherwise attainable are more scanty than of many of his contemporaries far inferior to him in intellectual powers and in public services."

Mason received a small, albeit belated, measure of recognition for his monumental contributions to his state and nation when, in April 2002, the National Park Service dedicated a modest George Mason Memorial in a secluded corner of the National Mall in Washington, D.C.

MAIN CONTRIBUTIONS OF GEORGE MASON

Mason was the author of the Fairfax Resolves in July 1774, which articulated the colonists' constitutional claims against the British.

He was a delegate to the Virginia Convention of 1776 where he was the principal draftsman of the Commonwealth's influential Declaration of Rights, adopted June 12, 1776, and first constitution following independence, adopted June 29, 1776. Both documents were models used by other states.

He was a Virginia delegate to and one of the most valuable members of the Constitutional Convention of 1787. He became a leading critic of the proposed Constitution, in part because it lacked a bill of rights, and led the campaign to defeat its ratification.

From the Pen of George Mason

A DECLARATION *of* RIGHTS *made by the representatives of the good people of* Virginia, *assembled in full and free Convention; which rights do pertain to them, and their posterity, as the basis and foundation of government.*

1. THAT all men are by nature equally free and independent, and have certain inherent rights, of which, when they enter into a state of society, they cannot, by any compact, deprive or divest their posterity; namely, the enjoyment of life and liberty, with the means of acquiring and possessing property, and pursuing and obtaining happiness and safety.

2. That all power is vested in, and consequently derived from, the people; that magistrates are their trustees and servants, and at all time amenable to them.

3. That government is, or ought to be, instituted for the common benefit, protection, and security, of the people, nation, or community, of all the various modes and forms of government that is best, which is capable of producing the greatest degree of happiness and safety, and is most effectually secured against the danger of mal-administration; and that whenever any government shall be found inadequate or contrary

to these purposes, a majority of the community hath an indubitable, unalienable, and indefeasible right, to reform, alter, or abolish it, in such manner as shall be judged conducive to the publick weal.

4. That no man, or set of men, are entitled to exclusive or separate emoluments or privileges from the community, but in consideration of publick services; which, not being descendible, neither ought the offices of magistrate, legislator, or judge, to be hereditary.

5. That the legislative and executive powers of the state should be separate and distinct from the judiciary; and that the members of the two first may be restrained from oppression, by feeling and participating the burthens of the people, they should, at fixed periods, be reduced to a private station, return into that body from which they were originally taken, and the vacancies be supplied by frequent, certain, and regular elections, in which all, or any part of the former members, to be again eligible, or ineligible, as the laws shall direct.

6. That elections of members to serve as representatives of the people, in assembly, ought to be free; and that all men, having sufficient evidence of permanent common interest with, and attachment to, the community, have the right of suffrage, and cannot be taxed or deprived of their property for publick uses without their own consent, or that of their representatives so elected, nor bound by any law to which they have not, in like manner, assented, for the publick good.

7. That all power of suspending laws, or the execution of laws, by any authority without consent of the representatives of the people, is injurious to their rights, and ought not to be exercised.

8. That in all capital or criminal prosecutions a man hath a right

to demand the cause and nature of his accusation, to be confronted with the accusers and witnesses, to call for evidence in his favour, and to a speedy trial by an impartial jury of his vicinage, without whose unanimous consent he cannot be found guilty, nor can he be compelled to give evidence against himself; that no man be deprived of his liberty except by the law of the land, or the judgment of his peers.

9. That excessive bail ought not to be required, nor excessive fines imposed, nor cruel and unusual punishments inflicted.

10. That general warrants, whereby any officer or messenger may be commanded to search suspected places without evidence of a fact committed, or to seize any person or persons not named, or whose offence is not particularly described and supported by evidence, are grievous and oppressive, and ought not to be granted.

11. That in controversies respecting property, and in suits between man and man, the ancient trial by jury is preferable to any other, and ought to be held sacred.

12. That the freedom of the press is one of the great bulwarks of liberty, and can never be restrained but by despotick governments.

13. That a well regulated militia, composed of the body of the people, trained to arms, is the proper, natural, and safe defence of a free state; that standing armies, in time of peace, should be avoided, as dangerous to liberty: and that, in all cases, the military should be under strict subordination to, and governed by, the civil power.

14. That the people have a right to uniform government; and therefore, that no government separate from, or independent of, the government of *Virginia*, ought to be erected or established within the limits thereof.

15. That no free government, or the blessing of liberty, can be preserved to any people but by a firm adherence to justice, moderation, temperance, frugality, and virtue, and by frequent recurrence to fundamental principles.

16. That religion, or the duty which we owe to our CREATOR, and the manner of discharging it, can be directed only by reason and conviction, not by force or violence, and therefore all men are equally entitled to the free exercise of religion, according to the dictates of conscience; and that it is the mutual duty of all to practice Christian forbearance, love, and charity, towards each other.

–George Mason, "Virginia Declaration of Rights,"

(June 12, 1776)

RECOMMENDED READING

Broadwater, Jeff. *George Mason: Forgotten Founder* (Chapel Hill: University of North Carolina Press, 2006).

Miller, Helen Hill. *George Mason: Gentleman Revolutionary* (Chapel Hill: University of North Carolina Press, 1975).

Rowland, Kate Mason. *The Life of George Mason, 1725-1792* 2 vols. (New York: G.P. Putnam's Sons, 1892).

Rutland, Robert A. *George Mason: Reluctant Statesman* (Baton Rouge: Louisiana State University Press, 1961).

"In adopting a republican form of government, I not only took it as a man does his wife, for better or for worse, but what few men do with their wives, I took it knowing all its bad qualities. Neither ingratitude, therefore, nor slander can disappoint expectation nor excite surprise. If, in arduous circumstances, the voice of my country should call for my services, and I have the well-founded belief, that they can be useful, they shall certainly be rendered; but I hope that no such circumstances will arise, and in the mean time, 'pleas'd let me trifle life away.'"

–Gouverneur Morris to John Dickenson, May 23, 1803

"It is not easy to be wise for all times, not even for the present – much less for the future; and those who judge of the past must recollect that, when it was present, the present was future."

–Gouverneur Morris to Robert Walsh, February 5, 1811

GOUVERNEUR MORRIS
(1752-1816)

JOHN K. BUSH

Gouverneur Morris helped draft the New York Constitution of 1777, and according to James Madison, "the finish given to the style and arrangement of the [U.S.] constitution fairly belongs to the pen of Mr. Morris." He served briefly in the Continental Congress but in his short tenure he played a critical role in supplying the Continental Army at Valley Forge and signed the Articles of Confederation. From 1781 through 1784 Morris was the Assistant Superintendent of Finance for the Continental Congress. President Washington appointed him as America's first official secret agent overseas (1788) and the U.S. Minister to France (1792-94). He also served as a U.S. Senator from New York from 1800-1803. After having many love interests, Morris was the last Founder to marry.

On January 31, 1752, Gouverneur Morris was born into a prominent New York family at their manoral estate, Morrisania, which is now part of the Bronx in New York City. He graduated from King's College (today Columbia University) at the age of sixteen, and afterwards apprenticed to be a lawyer. Morris recorded that he tried to model himself "after some persons who cut a figure in the law." He had an "irrepressible tendency to be flippant when he should be serious," as one biographer put it. But a sharp tongue did not impede his many successful business ventures.

When the War for Independence erupted, Morris's family split sharply. He joined with his half-brother, Lewis, who signed the Declaration of Independence. Morris wrote his Loyalist mother across enemy lines that he must be "called a rebel" for "sentiments . . . not fashionable among the folks you see." In February 1776, a New York regiment rejected Morris's application to serve as a colonel, probably because his right arm was withered–the result of a scalding from an accident in his youth. Morris apparently lost the commission to a person of lower social rank. He complained to his brother that "a herd of mechanics are preferred before the best families in the colony," but rationalized that "my little abilities [are] more adapted to the deliberations of the cabinet than the glorious labors of the field."

Morris's assessment proved correct. By the age of twenty-five he was serving in New York's Fourth Provincial Congress, which adopted the New York Constitution of 1777. He made a motion to urge future legislatures to abolish slavery and argued that "[t]he rights of human nature and our holy religion loudly call upon us to dispense the blessings of freedom to all mankind." Unfortunately, the motion failed, but it furthered a movement that eventually would lead to abolition in New York.

> "Morris should be remembered for his antislavery expressions in the Convention of 1787 and many other contributions to the final product of that convention."
>
> –Christopher Collier

In January 1778, Morris took his seat as one of New York's delegates to the Continental Congress. He served on a committee that traveled to Valley Forge and procured supplies for the Continental forces under

General George Washington. Morris literally begged provisions for them, as in a letter written to New York Governor George Clinton, which described "the American army, in the heart of America . . . on the point of deserting, having nothing to eat." Morris referred to the days of war as "the seed time of glory as of freedom," and became one of Washington's closest friends. Morris wrote that he was "an advocate for the army" who "loved them from acquaintance with some individuals and for the sufferings which as a body they had bravely and patiently endured."

In the spring of 1780, Morris's left leg was amputated after a runaway carriage accident, and he used a peg leg for the rest of his life. A day after the surgery, a friend tried to cheer him up with musings about good things Providence must have in mind for one who loses a limb. Morris responded, "My good sir, you argue the matter so handsomely and point out the advantages of being without legs, that I am almost tempted to part with the other."

Morris quipped about anything and anyone–not a good trait for a politician. Another delegate wrote that he was "like the elephant in war" who is "more destructive to his friends than to his antagonists." Not surprisingly, he lost his bid for reelection to the Continental Congress. From 1781 through 1784 he was the Assistant Superintendent of Finance, serving as the "right-hand man" to the "Financier" of the Revolution, Robert Morris (no relation).

After the War for Independence, the ensuing struggle for "a more perfect Union"–a phrase Morris would later add to the Constitution's preamble–again called Gouverneur Morris into public service. In the Continental Congress, he had signed the Articles of Confederation, which governed the country when, as Morris observed, "[t]he state of

America was suspended by a hair." He understood the importance of a stronger central government for the new republic to survive, and accordingly agreed to serve as one of Pennsylvania's delegates at the Constitutional Convention of 1787.

Morris liked to talk – a "brilliant talker," the historian Henry Adams would emphasize, "whose oratory was apt to verge on the domain of melodrama." In the Constitutional Convention, he made 173 speeches, more than any other delegate, and earned the nickname of "the eternal speaker." An admirer wrote that Morris's "language" was "eloquent" and "animated," but a detractor described him as "fickle and inconstant – never pursuing one train of thinking – nor ever regular."

Contemporary scholars are less critical of Morris's verbosity. Daniel L. Dreisbach calls him "one of the most influential" delegates who "made monumental contributions to the final document." For example, Morris, along with James Wilson, promoted "a strong chief executive within the necessary limits demanded by a republican form of government," as Christopher Wolf observes.

Morris also is noted for what he opposed at the Constitutional Convention. He called slavery a "nefarious institution" and "the curse of heaven on the states where it prevailed." He unsuccessfully tried to defeat a constitutional provision that would be eliminated after the Civil War, which counted each slave as 3/5 of a person in calculating a state's population for representation in the House of Representatives and the Electoral College.

Notwithstanding that he lost on slavery issues, Morris was "[o]ne of three who dominated debate," Carol Berkin writes. Scott Gerber concurs that "Morris is probably third in importance in framing the

Constitution." Indeed, as chief editor of the document, Morris's contributions were no mere window dressing. For example, he began the Preamble with the words "We the people" rather than "We the states," a choice that emphasized that the Constitution was a compact between each citizen as opposed to the states. "Those three words may be his greatest legacy," his biographer Richard Brookhiser concludes. James Madison wrote: "The finish given to the style and arrangement of the constitution fairly belongs to the pen of Mr. Morris. A better choice could not have been made, as the performance of the task proved. The talents and taste of the author were stamped on the face of it."

> "The language of the U.S. Constitution would be much poorer if it were not for the words of Gouverneur Morris."
> –Ryan J. Barilleaux

Curiously, for the man who was called "the foremost publicist of the Continental Congress," Morris was reluctant to expound in writing on the Constitutional Convention. During the debate, he wrote, "my mind was too much occupied with the interests of our country to keep notes of what we had done." In 1788, Morris declined Alexander Hamilton's request for Morris to help write the essays that would become *The Federalist Papers*. He would later claim, "It is not possible for me to recollect with precision all that passed in the Convention while we were framing the Constitution, and, if I could, it is most probable that meaning may have been conceived from incidental expressions different from that which they were intended to convey, and very different from the fixed opinions of the speaker."

Though he could turn a phrase better than most, Morris preferred action to words. He was soon off to Europe, where he conducted a secret mission in London on behalf of President Washington. He also tried, but failed, to organize a group of international investors to purchase all of the American war debt owed to France. He speculated heavily in securities and land in Europe and America. His "breathtakingly brassy" business dealings, combined with his polarizing personality, made him a controversial person for President Washington to appoint as U.S. Minister to France in 1792. He was barely confirmed by the U.S. Senate. Washington explained to Morris:

> "Whilst your abilities, knowledge in the affairs of this country, and disposition to serve it were adduced, asserted on one hand, you were charged on the other hand, with levity, and imprudence of conversation and conduct. It was urged, that your habit of expression, indicated a hauteur disgusting to those who happen to differ from you in sentiment; . . . [T]he promptitude with which your brilliant, and lively imagination is displayed, allows too little time for deliberation, and correction; and is the primary cause of those sallies which too often offend, and of that ridicule of characters which begets enmity not easy to be forgotten, but which might easily be avoided if it was under the control of more caution and prudence."

Washington nonetheless expressed confidence that Morris would bring more prudence to bear in his conduct.

But Washington knew from personal experience that Morris was unpredictable. Once, Hamilton had promised Morris the finest dinner for a dozen friends if he would greet the ever formal Washington with a slap on the back. Supposedly Morris clapped his hand on Washington's shoulder and exclaimed, "My dear general, how happy I am to see you look so well." Washington immediately removed Morris's hand, stepped back, and gave him the coldest stare. "Oh, that look!" Morris later recalled. "The majesty of the American people was before me. How I wished the floor would open and swallow me!"

As U.S. Minister to France, Morris advised King Louis XVI on how to deal with revolutionaries. He later stored some of the monarch's treasure in his desk for safe keeping and aided the royal family in one of their ill-fated attempts to escape the country. Morris also hid in his home French aristocrats who were targeted for execution. He kept a diary and wrote many letters that are among the best primary sources for understanding the French Revolution.

Legend has it that Morris's peg leg saved his life on one occasion in Paris. A mob halted his carriage and was about to drag him out and maul him. "An aristocrat!" they exclaimed in their native language. Morris then supposedly shouted in accented French while brandishing his wooden appendage: "An aristocrat! Yes, truly, who lost his leg in the cause of American liberty!" That silenced the crowd.

To his credit, Morris remained at his diplomatic post well after most ambassadors had fled the terror of Paris. Many American leaders faulted him for being too friendly with the royal family and the aristocratic elements of France, but in retrospect, many of his observations regarding the excesses of the French Revolution proved accurate. He correctly predicted the rise of Napoleon Bonaparte and the threat to peace posed by the expansionist French Empire. Morris helped implement Washington's policy of strict neutrality between England and France when many sought to tilt the balance of America's allegiance towards the latter.

After being recalled as ambassador for refusing to fully embrace the French revolutionary government, Morris took a long vacation, touring the Continent from 1795 through 1798. In 1799, he returned to America where he rebuilt his family's Morrisania estate and resumed his legal practice. From 1800 to 1803, he served as a U.S. Senator from New York. He was not reelected, but he refused to retire. In 1804, he helped found the New York Historical Society; in 1807, he served on a commission that planned the street grid for New York City; and in 1811, he was one of three commissioners who proposed the Erie Canal.

At the age of 57, Morris also undertook a new venture of a very personal sort–he married Anne Cary Randolph. He had had many love interests through the years, and many people were surprised when he became the last Founder to marry. Some relatives disapproved of his spouse. He replied to one such critic that "if the world were to live with my wife, I should certainly have consulted its taste; but as that happens not to be the case, I thought I might, without offending others, endeavor to suit myself." Mr. and Mrs. Morris had a son, Gouverneur Morris II, who would become a railroad magnate.

"One of three who dominated debate at the Constitutional Convention."

–Carol Berkin

Morris was a staunch Federalist and a fierce opponent of Presidents Thomas Jefferson and James Madison. He wrote that he and Jefferson "differ in our system of politics" and remarked that Jefferson was "cold as a frog." Morris minced no words as to Madison either, stating that he was "unfit for the station of President." He believed a report he heard that "Mr. Jefferson and Mr. Madison . . . are determined on going to war with England as soon as they can bring public opinion up to that measure." Like other Federalists, he was critical of "Mr. Madison's War"–i.e. the War of 1812. Many Federalists took their anti-war stance to an extreme, calling a meeting in Hartford, Connecticut, to plan secession of the northeastern states from the Union. Morris sympathized with the secessionists for a period, but he eventually concluded that their divisive objective was wrong.

By the time of his death in 1816, Morris again supported union of the states and expressed renewed faith in the Constitution. He also lost much of his partisan fervor. A few months before he passed away, Morris told a gathering of Federalists not to be so antagonistic towards the Democratic Republicans, stating "But, gentlemen, let us forget party, and think of our country. That country embraces both parties. We must endeavor, therefore, to save and benefit both."

MAIN CONTRIBUTIONS OF GOUVERNEUR MORRIS

Morris helped arrange supplies for the Continental Army and maintained the finances of the Continental Congress in the American Revolution.

A man who could turn a phrase, Morris spoke more than any other delegate at the Constitutional Convention and gave speeches remembered for both what they achieved (e.g., strong power for the executive branch) and what they did not (abolition of slavery). He was the chief editor of the U.S. Constitution.

Morris served as U.S. Minister to France during the French Revolution.

From the Pen of Gouverneur Morris

Preamble to the U.S. Constitution
We the People of the United States in order to form a more perfect Union, establish Justice, insure domestic Tranquility, provide for the common defence, promote the general Welfare, and secure the Blessings of Liberty to ourselves and our Posterity, do ordain and establish this Constitution of the United States of America.

RECOMMENDED READING

Richard Brookhiser, *Gentleman Revolutionary: Gouverneur Morris – The Rake Who Wrote the Constitution* (New York: Free Press, 2003).

Melanie Randolph Miller, *Gouverneur Morris & the French Revolution: Envoy to the Terror* (Dulles, VA: Potomac Books, Inc., 2005).

William Howard Adams, *Gouverneur Morris: An Independent Life* (New Haven, CT: Yale University Press, 2003).

James J. Kirschke, *Gouverneur Morris: Author, Statesman, and Man of the World* (New York: Thomas Dunne Books, 2005).

"To me it appears important that the American government be preserved as it is, until mature experience shall very plainly point out very useful amendments to our constitution; that we steadily repel all foreign influence and interference, and with good faith and liberality treat all nations as friends in peace, and as enemies in war; neither meddling with their affairs, nor permitting them to meddle with ours. These are the primary objects of my policy. The secondary ones are more numerous, such as, to be always prepared for war, to cultivate peace, to promote religion, industry, tranquility, and useful knowledge, and to secure to all the quiet enjoyment of their rights, by wise and equal laws irresistibly executed. I do not expect that mankind will, before the millennium, be what they ought to be; and therefore, in my opinion, every political theory which does not regard them as being what *they are*, will probably prove delusive."

–John Jay to Benjamin Vaughan, August 31, 1797

"Liberty and reformation may run mad, and madness of any kind is no blessing. I nevertheless think, that there may be a time for reformation, and a time for change, as well as for other things; all that I contend for is, that they be done soberly, by sober and discreet men, and in due manner, measure, and proportion. It may be said, that this cannot always be the case. It is true, and we can only regret it. We must take men and things as they are, and act accordingly; that is, circumspectly."

–John Jay to William Vaughan, May 26, 1797

JOHN JAY
(1745-1829)

JONATHAN DEN HARTOG

John Jay was a significant actor in the American Founding, serving in many roles and offices. During the Revolution he worked in New York government and was a delegate to both the First and Second Continental Congresses. In 1779, Congress sent him to Europe as Minister to Spain and later appointed him to be one of the three American commissioners who negotiated the Peace of Paris which ended the war. He wrote persuasively and acted effectively to secure the ratification of the Constitution. Under the new government he became the first Chief Justice of the Supreme Court. When war with England threatened in the 1790s, President Washington sent Jay to negotiate with England, and the end result—the Jay Treaty—helped keep the peace. After serving as New York's governor, Jay retired from public life in 1801. His thirty years of service had done much to help the new nation come into existence and become a stable republic.

Jay was a reluctant revolutionary. His background, temperament, and legal training all inclined against siding with the Patriot cause, but that was exactly what Jay did. Born in 1745, Jay was raised in a family with a strong Huguenot (French Protestant) ancestry, yet one which was also eager to take on English traits and find a place in the commercial realm of colonial New York. After graduating from King's College (today Columbia University), he studied law and was admitted to the New York bar in 1768. In 1774 he married Sarah Livingston, daughter of the prominent political leader William Livingston. As the conflict with Great Britain escalated, John became more involved in public meetings, and New York sent him as a delegate to the First Continental Congress at the age of twenty-nine.

In the Continental Congress, Jay advocated a policy of cautious yet firm resistance to Great Britain. John Adams found him "a Man of Wit, well-informed, a good Speaker, and an elegant writer." Jay drafted the Congress's "Address to the People of Great Britain," a conciliatory piece which invited Britain to rethink its American policies. Even after military conflict broke out at Lexington and Concord in April 1775, Jay continued to hope for reconciliation. In the Second Continental Congress, he worked with John Dickinson to draft the Olive Branch Petition to George III–a last attempt at compromise that the King refused even to receive.

Recalled to New York, Jay filled a number of state offices. He had given up hope for peace, believing that "our country was prompted and impelled to independence by necessity and not by choice," and so he directed the state's endorsement of the Declaration of Independence. Jay next helped draft the state's first constitution. At the same time he wrote "An Address of the Convention of the Representatives of the State of New-York, to Their Constituents," which encouraged New Yorkers to continue fighting, even as the war seemed to be going against the Patriots. He also had some responsibility for the organization of New York's militias and even oversaw some spies behind British lines. When New York state established its judicial system, Jay was named its first Chief Justice. Throughout his life, he believed that established law was necessary for order and good government and sought to advance the rule of law.

> "Given the astonishing range of his accomplishment—president of Continental Congress, minister to France and Spain, co-author of the Federalist Papers, first Chief Justice of the Supreme Court, Governor of New York, leader of Federalist Party, early opponent of slavery—it is amazing that Jay is so little known. He deserves better."
>
> — Wilfred McClay

Arm an alliance with Spain or at least gain additional loans to support the war effort. Jay approached the assignment pessimistically, and he was not disappointed as the Spanish court virtually ignored him. He was relieved when Congress sent him to Paris to assist John Adams and Benjamin Franklin in negotiating the terms of the Peace Treaty with the British. Jay and Adams collaborated closely in the talks with both Great Britain and America's ally France. They decided to go against the wishes of the Comte de Vergennes, the French foreign minister, and sought a separate peace with Great Britain. Their determined, canny diplomacy gained the United States the best possible terms and laid the groundwork for later westward expansion.

After he returned to the United States in 1784, Jay found that he had been elected once again to Congress. Congress appointed him as its Secretary of Foreign Affairs, which made him responsible for all of the Confederation's diplomatic matters. He bemoaned the way he often had to act from a position of weakness rather than strength. In a series of letters to George Washington, John Adams, and Thomas Jefferson, Jay delineated the failures of the Articles of Confederation and the need for constitutional reforms. Notably, he advocated the creation of an independent chief executive and judiciary and a system of checks and balances. Jay thus welcomed the eventual calling of the

Constitutional Convention.

New York chose to send only a small delegation to Philadelphia in 1787, leaving John out of the Convention, but he was nevertheless pleased with the proposed Constitution. He fought for the document's ratification in New York, most significantly by joining with Alexander Hamilton and James Madison to write *The Federalist Papers*. He was responsible for *Federalist* numbers 2, 3, 4, 5, and 64, which present a hopeful argument for the adoption of the Constitution. He contended that it would secure pre-existing American unity and lay the groundwork for further national success. Jay also wrote the very important "Address to the People of the State of New York, on the Subject of the Constitution." This single pamphlet helped sway opinion in New York, which was in a critical position for determining the direction of the nation, and it was republished throughout the country. John Adams recognized that Jay's effort in support of the Constitution was "of more importance than any of the rest, indeed of almost as much weight as all the rest." More recently, the scholar Robert Ferguson observed in his 2004 book *Reading the Early Republic* that "the ambiance of his [Jay's] writings managed to capture and then hold the imagination of the age."

Jay was also a central figure in the New York Ratification Convention. His strategizing and rhetoric took a convention that began opposed to the Constitution and actually moved the delegates to approve it. A sympathetic observer of the scene wrote, "Mr. [Jay]'s reasoning is weighty as gold, polished as silver, and strong as steel." Without Jay's skill and hard work, New York may not have ratified the Constitution, and the new government may never have come into existence.

With the new government formed, President-elect Washington

offered Jay his choice of offices, and Jay requested the Chief Justiceship of the Supreme Court. Washington approved, commenting that Jay possessed the "talents, knowledge, and integrity which are so necessary" for the office. Jay wanted this position because he continued to believe that a solid legal order was essential for the healthy functioning of a republican government. As Chief Justice, Jay was responsible for overseeing the lower federal courts, annually riding circuit (in New England, then later in the Southern states), addressing grand juries, and hearing cases that rose to the Supreme Court. In his jurisprudence, Jay worked to shape national law and policy, as well as to support the nation against foreign powers.

In the 1790s, the United States had to confront problems originating from Europe. The French Revolution had begun in 1789 and soon produced international conflict. With France and Great Britain locked in war, America struggled to maintain its neutrality. Conflicts with Great Britain over neutral sailing rights, access to Caribbean ports, remaining British forts in the Northwest Territory, and British encouragement of Indian attacks threatened to drag America into war. To avert such a calamity, President Washington sent Jay as a special emissary to Britain in 1794. Jay negotiated a treaty which, although it did not gain everything Americans hoped for, was probably the best that could have been obtained under the circumstances. Returning home, Jay was subjected to considerable abuse by the treaty's critics. After much political wrangling and the determined efforts of President Washington and his allies, however, the Senate approved the Treaty. Jay had succeeded in keeping the nation out of war and buying the young republic additional years of peace in which to mature. His reputation, however, suffered under the intense criticism.

In 1795, New York elected Jay as governor, so he resigned his seat on the Supreme Court to serve the next six years in that post. He largely dealt with local matters, such as controlling a Yellow Fever outbreak and making sure that harbor defenses were in place. Jay's actions also overlapped with increasing national excitement, and in the fever for war with France in 1798, he called up the New York militia. Jay's other accomplishment as governor was to pass a gradual emancipation bill, which eventually ended slavery in New York. After almost thirty years of uninterrupted service, Jay retired from public life in 1801.

"Because of his extensive diplomatic service to the new nation, his lead role as an author of the New York Constitution of 1777, his writings during the ratification controversy of 1787-1788 and his instrumental role in New York's vote to ratify the Constitution, and finally his faithful service as the nation's first Chief Justice in the neglected pre-Marshall period of the Supreme Court's history, Jay deserves recognition as one of the most valuable and constructive members of the group whom we call the Founding Fathers."

—R.B. Bernstein

During his career, Jay's principles were clearly republican and Federalist. He strongly supported the American experiment of republican self-government under law, as opposed to the monarchies which then filled Europe. Jay was also a Federalist, not only a supporter of the Constitution but a member of the Federalist political party which flourished in the 1790s and into the 1800s. As his correspondence and speeches indicate, Jay's political principles for the new nation began with his support of constitutional government.

Having labored to put the Constitution in place, Jay believed it—rather than the loudest voices in a mob—should be the guiding principle of American government. Using an extended metaphor, he told his friend William Vaughan:

> "I should not think that man wise, who should employ his time in endeavouring to contrive a shoe that would fit every foot; and they do not appear to me much more wise, who expect to devise a government that would suit every nation. I have no objections to men's mending or changing their own shoes, but object to their insisting on mending or changing mine."

In contrast to the utopian schemes of the French Revolution, Jay was quite content with the constitutional "shoe" produced in 1787, believing the political cobblers had done their job well. Foreign interference was unwelcome, especially from those who did not know American circumstances or who offered ideologically "pre-cut" soles. Jay approved of occasional constitutional amendment, but only when it was prudent and well thought out. Reform was best done gradually.

Jay believed democracy was necessary in a constitutional republic, but it should be tempered and bounded. As he told a friend, "Too many...love pure democracy dearly. They seem not to consider that pure democracy, like pure rum, easily produces intoxication, and with it a thousand mad pranks and fooleries." He preferred an orderly society with its tone set by "sober and discreet" men. Supporting such an orderly society was morality and religious belief, and Jay came to believe increasingly in the importance of religious faith in the new republic. Finally, Jay hoped that such an orderly society would allow for the cultural and moral improvement of its citizens. If the country followed these guidelines, Jay believed the result would be a successful, flourishing republic.

Jay retired to his country home in Bedford, Westchester County. There he had much time to reflect on the revolutionary era. His lifelong Protestant Christian beliefs also grew more pronounced in retirement. Faith helped him deal with the loss of both his wife and a daughter. It also impelled Jay to a different type of service: the presidency of the American Bible Society. The American Bible Society was committed to blanketing the nation with the Protestant Scriptures, to be printed "without note or comment" as a means of converting the country. Jay presided over the organization–even though he had little to do with its daily operation–from 1821 to 1825. Jay died peacefully in 1829, having outlived all the Founders except Charles Carroll.

With such an extended and significant service, Jay's status as a "forgotten" Founder is shocking. As the historian Wilfred McClay observed, "Given the astonishing range of his accomplishment…it is amazing that Jay is so little known. He deserves better." Historian R.B. Bernstein suggested that this lack of recognition came about because Jay never signed any of the major Founding documents. Biographer Walter Stahr argued that Jay was more conservative and more religious than many of the other Founders, which explains the lack of attention he has received. I would add that Jay's association with the Federalist Party has hurt him. He was a central figure in a political party that had disappeared by 1820, having failed to create a party tradition in which Jay could be remembered. Whatever the case, it is indisputable that without Jay's many services to the new nation, the United States would have lacked a great, effective talent and may have taken a very different course than it did. Jay helped set the nation on a path of stable, constitutional, non-revolutionary political development.

MAIN CONTRIBUTIONS OF JOHN JAY

Jay forcefully advocated for the ratification of the Constitution. He joined with Alexander Hamilton and James Madison to write the *Federalist Papers*. He also penned the significant "Address to the People of the State of New York, on the Subject of the Constitution."

Jay served as the first Chief Justice of the Supreme Court. As Chief Justice, he worked to strengthen the federal government's powers in relation to the states and foreign nations.

Jay acted as President Washington's emissary to Great Britain in 1794-95. He negotiated the Jay Treaty, which kept the United States out of war with Britain by addressing several areas of tension between the two nations.

From the Pen of John Jay

"Nothing is more certain than the indispensable necessity of government, and it is equally undeniable, that whenever and however it is instituted, the people must cede to it some of their natural rights in order to vest it with requisite powers. It is well worthy of consideration therefore, whether it would conduce more to the interest of the people of America that they should, to all general purposes, be one nation, under one federal government, or that they should divide themselves into separate confederacies, and give to the head of each the same kind of powers which they are advised to place in one national government.

It has until lately been a received and uncontradicted opinion that the prosperity of the people of America depended on their continuing firmly united, and the wishes, prayers, and efforts of our best and wisest citizens have been constantly directed to that object. But politicians now appear, who insist that this opinion is erroneous, and that instead of looking for safety and happiness in union, we ought to seek it in a division of the States into distinct confederacies or sovereignties. However extraordinary this new doctrine may appear, it nevertheless has its advocates; and certain characters who were much opposed to it formerly, are at present of the number. Whatever may be the arguments or inducements which have wrought this change in the sentiments and declarations of these gentlemen, it certainly would not be wise in the people at large to adopt these new political tenets without being fully convinced that they are founded in truth and sound policy.

It has often given me pleasure to observe that independent America was not composed of detached and distant territories, but that one connected, fertile, widespreading country was the portion of our western sons of liberty. Providence has in a particular manner blessed it with a variety of soils and productions, and watered it with innumerable streams, for the delight and accommodation of its inhabitants. A succession of navigable waters forms a kind of chain round its borders, as if to bind it together; while the most noble rivers in the world, running at convenient distances, present them with highways for the easy communication of friendly aids, and the mutual transportation and exchange of their various commodities.

With equal pleasure I have as often taken notice that Providence has been pleased to give this one connected country to one united people – a people descended from the same ancestors, speaking the same language, professing the same religion, attached to the same principles of government, very similar in their manners and customs, and who, by their joint counsels, arms, and efforts, fighting side by side throughout a long and bloody war, have nobly established general liberty and independence.

This country and this people seem to have been made for each other, and it appears as if it was the design of Providence, that an inheritance so proper and convenient for a band of brethren, united to each other by the strongest ties, should never be split into a number of unsocial, jealous, and alien sovereignties.

Similar sentiments have hitherto prevailed among all orders and denominations of men among us. To all general purposes we have uniformly been one people each individual citizen everywhere enjoying the same national rights, privileges, and protection. As a nation we have made peace and war; as a nation we have vanquished our common enemies; as a nation we have formed alliances, and made treaties, and entered into various compacts and conventions with foreign states.

A strong sense of the value and blessings of union induced the people, at a very early period, to institute a federal government to preserve and perpetuate it.

…This [Constitutional] convention, composed of men who possessed the confidence of the people, and many of whom had become highly distinguished by their Patriotism, virtue and wisdom, in times which tried the minds and hearts of men, undertook the arduous task. In the mild season of peace, with minds unoccupied by other subjects, they passed many months in cool, uninterrupted, and daily consultation; and finally, without having been awed by power, or influenced by any passions except love for their country, they presented and recommended to the people the plan produced by their joint and very unanimous councils.

…It is worthy of remark that not only the first, but every succeeding Congress, as well as the late convention, have invariably joined with the people in thinking that the prosperity of America depended on its Union. To preserve and perpetuate it was the great object of the people in forming that convention, and it is also the great object of the plan which the convention has advised them to adopt. With what propriety, therefore, or for what good purposes, are attempts at this particular period made by some men to depreciate the importance of the Union? Or why is it suggested that three or four confederacies would be better than one? I am persuaded in my own mind that the people have always thought right on this subject, and that their universal and uniform attachment to the cause of the Union rests on great and weighty reasons, which I shall endeavor to develop and explain in some ensuing papers. They who promote the idea of substituting a number of distinct confederacies in the room of the plan of the convention, seem clearly to foresee that the rejection of it would put the continuance of the Union in the utmost jeopardy. That certainly would be the case, and I sincerely wish that it may be as clearly foreseen by every good citizen, that whenever the dissolution of the Union arrives, America will have reason to exclaim, in the words of the poet: "FAREWELL! A LONG FAREWELL TO ALL MY GREATNESS."

– John Jay, *The Federalist Papers*, Number 2 (1787)

RECOMMENDED READING

Stahr, Walter. *John Jay: Founding Father.* (NY: Hambledon and London, 2005).

Morris, Richard. *Witnesses at the Creation: Hamilton, Madison, Jay, and the Constitution.* (NY: Holt, Rinehart, and Winston, 1985).

Estes, Todd. *The Jay Treaty Debate, Public Opinion, and the Evolution of Early American Political Culture.* (Amherst: University of Massachusetts Press, 2006).

The John Jay Papers Project. **www.columbia.edu/cu/lweb/digital/jay**

"Philosophy may mislead you. Ask experience."

 "Minorities talk, majorities vote."

ROGER SHERMAN
(1721-1793)

MARK DAVID HALL

Roger Sherman was the only Founder to help draft and sign the Declaration and Resolves (1774), the Articles of Association (1774), the Declaration of Independence (1776), the Articles of Confederation (1777, 1778), and the Constitution (1787). He served more days in the Continental Congress than any other member, and he was on the five-man committee that wrote the Declaration of Independence. At the Federal Convention of 1787, he spoke more than any delegate but James Madison and was the driving force behind the Connecticut Compromise. As a Representative and Senator in the national legislature under the U.S. Constitution, he played critical roles in debates over the Bill of Rights, the assumption of state debts, and the establishment of a national bank. Even as he was helping to create and run a new nation, he served simultaneously in a variety of state offices.

Sherman was born in Stoughton, Massachusetts in 1721. Shortly after the death of his father in 1741, he moved to New Milford, Connecticut, where he worked as a cobbler, surveyor, and store owner. Sherman never attended college, but he taught himself advanced mathematics, and in 1750 he began publishing a popular almanac which was issued annually until 1761. He also taught himself law and was admitted to the Litchfield bar in 1754. As he prospered professionally, he was selected for a variety of local offices and was elected to several six month terms in the lower house of Connecticut's General Assembly.

In 1760, after the death of his first wife (with whom he had seven children), Sherman moved to New Haven. He opened a store next to Yale College and sold general merchandise, provisions, and books. Sherman married Rebecca Prescott three years later, and they had eight children. He was again elected to the lower house of the General Assembly, and in 1766 Connecticut voters chose him to be one of the twelve members of the upper house, or Council of Assistants. Traditionally, four Assistants were selected by the General Assembly to serve with the deputy governor as the judges on Connecticut's Superior Court. Sherman was appointed to this court in 1766, and he held both offices until he resigned from the legislature in 1785. He remained a Superior Court Judge until he became a member of the United States House of Representatives in 1789.

> "Sherman is the only person to have signed all the essential documents of the American Founding. That includes the Declaration of Independence, the Articles of Confederation, the Constitution, and the Bill of Rights. He was instrumental in both moderating Madison's nationalism at the Constitutional Convention and securing ratification of the Constitution and the Bill of Rights."
>
> —Gordon Lloyd

Beginning with the Stamp Act Crisis of 1765, Sherman was a consistent opponent of what he considered to be British abuses of power. As a member of the First Continental Congress in 1774, he helped draft and signed the Declaration and Resolves, which among other things declared:

"That the inhabitants of the English Colonies in North America, by the immutable laws of nature, the principles of the English constitution, and the several charters or compacts, have the following Rights:

Resolved: 1. That they are entitled to life, liberty, and property, and they have never ceded to any sovereign power whatever, a right to dispose of either without their consent. . . ."

The Congress went on to assert that Parliament had no authority to tax the colonies, although to Sherman's chagrin it conceded that it could regulate colonial trade.

In addition to declaring their rights and petitioning the king, the First Continental Congress passed the Articles of Association, whereby delegates agreed on behalf of their colonies not to import and consume goods from Great Britain or Ireland. The articles provided for the creation of committees in each county, city, and town to enforce the terms of the association. Sherman signed this agreement, and he later was moderator at the New Haven town meeting that formed the committee to implement the Articles in that city. He occasionally chaired this body, but pressing responsibilities in Congress necessitated frequent absences from New Haven.

In 1776, Sherman was the only delegate to serve on all three of the most important congressional committees: the Board of War, the committee to draft the Declaration of Independence (fellow members included Thomas Jefferson, John Adams, Benjamin Franklin, and

Robert Livingston), and the thirteen-member committee to draft what became the Articles of Confederation. He was intimately involved with the war effort and in writing the Articles but, unfortunately for his future fame, he was content for Jefferson to do most of the work on the Declaration. He was repeatedly selected to represent his state in the Continental and Confederation Congresses, eventually serving a total of 1,543 days.

Back in Connecticut, Sherman and the aptly named Richard Law accepted the task of revising *all* of Connecticut's statutes. To divide this huge endeavor, Sherman took statutes beginning with the letters A-L and Law took the rest. The two worked on the project throughout the summer and fall of 1783. The General Assembly reviewed their work and approved it with a few changes in January 1784. Among Sherman's contributions was a religious liberty statute entitled "An Act for securing the Rights of Conscience in Matters of Religion, to Christians of every Denomination in this State." The revisions also included a law providing for the gradual emancipation of children born to slaves in Connecticut after March 1, 1784.

In 1787, the General Assembly appointed Sherman, Oliver Ellsworth, and William Samuel Johnson to represent Connecticut in the Federal Constitutional Convention. No delegate had more experience in national government, and only one member–Benjamin Franklin–had more experience in politics than Sherman. In spite of his age, he spoke more times than anyone except James Madison.

Sherman arrived in Philadelphia convinced that the national government's powers needed to be strengthened, but he was also a firm supporter of both local and limited government. As such, he was shocked by Madison's proposals for a national legislature based upon proportional representation and possessing a general grant of power and the ability to veto state laws. Sherman tenaciously fought each of these ideas, eventually winning equal representation for states in the Senate, an enumeration of Congress's powers, and the elimination of the national government's ability to veto state laws. He was less successful in his opposition to a single, powerful executive who would be independent of the legislature.

Sherman's most significant contribution in Philadelphia was the "Great" or "Connecticut" Compromise. When it became apparent that the large states would not accept retaining the Articles' provision of one-state-one-vote, and the small states would not agree to proportional representation alone, Sherman helped craft the compromise whereby membership in the House of Representatives would be proportionally allocated based on state population while states would be represented equally in the Senate—initially with the senators to be chosen by the state legislatures. Without this compromise, it is unlikely the Constitution would have been ratified.

Sherman's contributions in the Federal Convention were neglected for many years, but scholars have recently gained a better appreciation for them. For instance, David Brian Robertson concludes in a 2005 article published in *The American Political Science Review* (the discipline's top journal), that Sherman often outmaneuvered Madison at the Constitutional Convention, and he suggests that the "political synergy between Madison and Sherman . . . very well may have been necessary for the Constitution's adoption."

After the Convention, Sherman returned to Connecticut where he wrote seven newspaper essays under the pseudonyms of "Countryman" and "A Citizen of New Haven" defending the Constitution. He was elected to represent New Haven at the state ratification convention where, according to one account, "all the objections to the Constitution vanished before the learning and eloquence of a Johnson, the genuine good sense and discernment of a Sherman, and the Demosthenian energy of an Ellsworth." The reporter may have been biased, but the sense of Federalist domination was accurate as indicated by the January 9, 1788 vote of 128-40 in favor of the Constitution. Connecticut thus became the fifth state to ratify the document.

In December of 1788, Sherman was elected to the House of Representatives, and in 1791, he was appointed to the U.S. Senate to fill the unexpired term of William Samuel Johnson. In Congress he engaged in debates over tariffs, the assumption of state debts, and the creation of a national bank. Although initially opposed to adding a bill of rights to the Constitution, Sherman served on the eleven-member House committee that drafted the amendments, was an active participant in debates over the specific provisions, and was a member of the six-person conference committee that put the amendments into their final form. As well, Sherman argued for placing the amendments after the original Constitution rather than interspersing them within the text as originally proposed by Madison. Sherman remained active in politics until his death on July 23, 1793.

"No individual was more directly and intimately involved in the major actions of the American Founding than Roger Sherman."
—Daniel L. Dreisbach

Sherman was held in high esteem by his contemporaries. In 1777 John Adams described him as "that old puritan, as honest as an angel, and as firm in the cause of American Independence as Mt. Atlas." Late in life, Patrick Henry remarked that Sherman and George Mason were "the greatest statesmen he ever knew." Thomas Jefferson, who was often at odds with both Adams and Henry, shared their admiration for Sherman. He once pointed Sherman out to a visitor and noted "[t]hat is Mr. Sherman of Connecticut, a man who never said a foolish thing in his life."

Jefferson's comment highlights Sherman's proclivity to bring a healthy dose of common sense to political deliberations. In the Constitutional Convention, Robert Yates recorded him as commenting: "I am not fond of speculation. I would rather proceed on experimental ground [i.e. on the ground of experience]." Similarly, in an essay defending the proposed Constitution, Sherman wrote, "Philosophy may mislead you. Ask experience." His contributions to crafting the Declaration and Resolves (1774), the Articles of Association (1774), the Declaration of Independence (1776), the Articles of Confederation (1777, 1778), the Constitution (1787), and the Bill of Rights (1789) all reflect his prudential approach to politics. Sherman was not a radical thinker, a great author, or a stirring orator–realities that diminished his contemporary and future fame. Nevertheless, as historian Jack N. Rakove comments in his Pulitzer Prize winning book *Original Meanings*, "America has had more Shermans in its politics than Madisons, and arguably too few of either, but it was the rivalry between their competing goals and political styles that jointly gave the Great Convention much of its drama and fascination–and also permitted its achievement." Scholars, teachers, and students who wish to understand America's Founding cannot afford to ignore the contributions of that old Connecticut Puritan, Roger Sherman.

MAIN CONTRIBUTIONS
OF ROGER SHERMAN

Sherman was the only person to sign the Declaration and Resolves (1774), the Articles of Association (1774), the Declaration of Independence (1776), the Articles of Confederation (1777, 1778), and the Constitution (1787).

Sherman played critical roles in drafting the Constitution and the Bill of Rights.

Sherman was actively involved in Connecticut state government, serving in the upper house of the General Assembly from 1766-1785 and on the Superior Court from 1766-1789. In 1783 he and Richard Law revised all of Connecticut's laws.

From the Pen of Roger Sherman

"As the happiness of a People, and the good Order of Civil Society, essentially depend upon Piety, Religion and Morality, it is the Duty of the Civil Authority to provide for the Support and Encouragement thereof; so as that Christians of every Denomination, demeaning themselves peaceably, and as good Subjects of the State, may be equally under the

Protection of the Laws: And as the People of this State have in general, been of one Profession in Matters of Faith, religious Worship, and the mode of settling and supporting the Ministers of the Gospel, they have by Law been formed into Ecclesiastical Societies, for the more convenient Support of their Worship and Ministry: And to the End that other Denominations of Christians who dissent from the Worship and Ministry so established and supported, may enjoy free Liberty of Conscience in the Matters aforesaid:

Be it enacted by the Governor, Council and Representatives, in General Court assembled, and by the Authority of the same, That no Persons in this State, professing the Christian Religion, who soberly and conscientiously dissent from the Worship and Ministry by Law established in the Society wherein they dwell, and attend public Worship by themselves, shall incur any Penalty for not attending the Worship and Ministry so established, on the Lord's-Day, or on account of their meeting together by themselves on said Day, for public Worship in a Way agreeable to their Consciences.

And be it further enacted by the Authority aforesaid, That all denominations of Christians differing in their religious Sentiments from the People of the established Societies in this State, whether of the Episcopal Church, or those Congregationalists called Separates, or of the People called Baptists, or Quakers, or any other Denomination who shall have formed themselves into distinct Churches or Congregations, and attend public Worship, and support the gospel Ministry in a Way agreeable to their Consciences and respective Professions; and all Persons who adhere to any of them, and dwell so near to any Place of their Worship that they can do ordinarily attend the same on the Sabbath, and contribute their due Proportion to the support of the Worship and Ministry where they so attend, whether such Place of Worship be within this, or any adjoining State, and produce a Certificate thereof from such Church or Congregation, signed by their Order, by the Minister or other Officer thereof, and lodge the same with the Clerk of the Society wherein such Person or Persons dwell, every such Person shall be exempted from being taxed for the support of the Worship and Ministry of said Society, so long as he or they shall continue so to attend and support public Worship with a different Church or Congregation as aforesaid.

And be it further enacted by the Authority aforesaid, That all such Protestant Churches and Congregations as different from the Worship and Ministry established as aforesaid, and who maintain and attend public Worship by themselves, shall have Liberty and Authority to use and exercise the same Powers and Privileges for maintaining and supporting their respective Ministers, and building and repairing their Meeting-Houses for the public Worship of God, as the Ecclesiastical Societies, constituted by Act of the General Assembly of this State by Law have and do exercise and enjoy; and in the same Manner may commence and hold their Meetings, and transact their Affairs, as Occasion may require for the Purpose aforesaid.

And all Persons shall be taxed for the support of the Ministry and other Charges of the Society wherein they dwell, who do not attend and help Support, any other public Worship; any thing in this Act notwithstanding.

And every Person claiming the benefit of this Act, shall be disqualified to vote in any Society Meeting, save only for granting Taxes for the support of Schools, and for the Establishment of

Rules and Regulations for Schools, and the Education of Children in them."

–Roger Sherman, From "An Act for securing the Rights of Conscience in Matters of Religion, to Christians of every Denomination in this State" (1784)

RECOMMENDED READING

Collier, Christopher. *Roger Sherman's Connecticut: Yankee Politics and the American Revolution.* (Middletown: Wesleyan University Press, 1971).

Boardman, Roger Sherman. *Roger Sherman: Signer and Statesman.* Philadelphia: (University of Pennsylvania Press, 1938).

Gerber, Scott. "Roger Sherman and the Bill of Rights." *Polity* 28 (Summer 1996): 521-40.

"It is a proposition too plain to be contested, that the constitution controls any legislative act repugnant to it. . . .[A]n act of the legislature repugnant to the constitution is void. . . . It is emphatically the province and duty of the judicial department to say what the law is."

–John Marshall, *Marbury v. Madison*, (1803)

"The government of the United States, then, though limited in its powers, is supreme; and its laws, when made in pursuance of the constitution, form the supreme law of the land, 'any thing in the constitution or laws of any State to the contrary notwithstanding.'"

–John Marshall, *McCulloch v. Maryland*, (1819)

"This power [over commerce], like all others vested in congress, is complete in itself, may be exercised to its utmost extent, and acknowledges no limitations, other than are prescribed in the constitution. . . . If, as has always been understood, the sovereignty of congress, though limited to specified objects, is plenary as to those objects, the power over commerce with foreign nations, and among the several states, is vested in congress as absolutely as it would be in a single government."

–John Marshall, *Gibbons v. Ogden*, (1824)

JOHN MARSHALL
(1755-1835)

HENRY J. ABRAHAM AND BARBARA A. PERRY

Matthew Franck has summarized John Marshall brilliantly as "A brave soldier in the Revolution, a brilliant lawyer, a leader in Virginia's ratification of the Constitution, an accomplished diplomat, congressman, and Secretary of State, John Marshall could have retired from public life in 1801 with a secure though minor place in the tale of the early Republic. But for the next three and a half decades, as Chief Justice of the United States, he had a more profound impact on American life than any other judge in our history. He established the Supreme Court's independence as a co-equal branch of government, enunciated and defended the essential principles of the American Union, and taught his contemporaries and posterity alike how to read and understand the United States Constitution– a task that amounted to the completion of the Founding."

One of the first actions John G. Roberts, Jr. took after being sworn in as Chief Justice in 2005 was to send an emissary to Richmond, Virginia, on a mission to procure John Marshall's judicial robe, displayed at his historic home. Roberts wanted to replicate the garment worn by his hero, known as "The Great Chief Justice." The Supreme Court's new leader could not have chosen a better role model on whom to pattern his attire or tenure.

Born near Germantown in 1755, on the frontier of colonial Virginia, John Marshall was the eldest of fifteen children. His parents and tutors provided most of young John's early education, but his schooling in human nature as the oldest sibling of such a large brood taught him leadership skills that would last a lifetime. Following the "shot heard round the world," at Lexington and Concord, which launched the American Revolution in 1775, Marshall and his father enlisted with the Culpeper Minute Men. John later served with a Virginia Continental Regiment, rising to the rank of captain. He led his men in the battles of Great Bridge, Brandywine, Germantown, and Monmouth Courthouse. He also suffered through the winter encampment at Valley Forge, emerging with a life-long admiration for George Washington, about whom he wrote a five-volume biography entitled *Life of George Washington.*

"John Marshall played a crucial role at key stages of the Founding."
—Ryan J. Barilleaux

After the War for Independence, Marshall studied with the renowned legal scholar, George Wythe, at the College of William and Mary. After acceptance to the bar, Marshall moved to Virginia's capital, Richmond, settling there with his wife Polly. They had ten children, six of whom survived to adulthood. Blessed with abundant intellectual skills, verbal talents, and charm, Marshall achieved success as an appellate lawyer in state and federal courts. His public service in Virginia's Council of State (1782-1784) and its House of Delegates (1782, 1784-1785, 1787-1788, 1795) confirmed his doubts about the competency of state government. Marshall became a staunch nationalist and member of the Federalist party, whose views he represented as an elected delegate to the Virginia convention that ratified the new federal Constitution in 1787. His lucid defense of the proposed federal judiciary contributed to the convention's adoption of the national system that governs the United States to this day.

An effective spokesman for President Washington's policies, Marshall received offers to appointive offices, but he rejected them to continue his lucrative law practice. When President John Adams asked him to serve on a diplomatic mission to revolutionary France, however, he accepted. As the United States attempted to maneuver between French and British hostilities, the assignment was particularly delicate. Marshall, and his two colleagues, Charles Cotesworth Pinckney and Elbridge Gerry, returned from France as heroes for refusing to pay a bribe to representatives of the French government. As a result, President Washington, now in retirement, prevailed upon Marshall to run for a seat in the U.S. House of Representatives from a Richmond district. He served there for less than a year (1799-1800), presenting moderate Federalist views in House debates.

In 1800 President Adams appointed Marshall Secretary of State. During his nine months in the cabinet, his duties included conducting American foreign policy, facilitating appointments to federal offices, and assisting the President in government administration while he was away from the nation's capital.

On January 20, 1801, John Adams, a lame-duck President since his defeat by Thomas Jefferson in 1800, nominated Marshall to serve as Chief Justice of the Supreme Court. One week later, the Senate approved the appointment unanimously, setting the stage for his 34½-year tenure on the highest court in the land. From 1801 to 1835, he authored 519 out of the 1,215 opinions issued by the Court, including over half of the 62 decisions the Justices handed down on constitutional questions. It is simply beyond dispute that Chief Justice Marshall, more than any other individual in the history of the Court, determined the developing character of America's federal constitutional system. He raised the Court from its lowly, if not discredited, position to a level of equality with the executive and the legislative branches, perhaps even to one of dominance during the heyday of his Chief Justiceship. Long after the Federalist party had faded from the political scene (John Adams was its last President), Marshall continued to write the party's nationalist philosophy into constitutional law. Adams could proudly and justly say, "[m]y gift of John Marshall to the people of the United States was the proudest act of my life. There is no act of my life on which I reflect with more pleasure. I have given to my country a judge equal to a Hale, a Holt, or a Mansfield."

Marshall handed down four of the most momentous decisions in the nation's history. *Marbury v. Madison* (1803) established the Supreme Court's power of judicial review over congressional acts and solidified the U.S. Constitution's supremacy. Events giving rise to this case began after Thomas Jefferson, a Republican, defeated President Adams's bid for reelection in 1800. Just prior to leaving office, Adams, a staunch Federalist, appointed a number of his party's loyalists to the federal bench. In response, the Jeffersonian Republicans in Congress repealed the Judiciary Act of 1800, which had created new circuit courts and judgeships. By the time Jefferson assumed the presidency, a number of Adams's commissions had been signed but not delivered. President Jefferson ordered his new Secretary of State, James Madison, not to deliver them. As a result, William Marbury, one of Adams nominees who had not received his commission, sued Madison and requested that the Supreme Court order him to deliver the commission. The Judiciary Act of 1789 provided the Court with authority to deliver this order (called a writ of *mandamus*). Marshall immediately recognized that the Jefferson Administration would ignore the Court's order. On the other hand, failure to grant the writ could be interpreted as a sign of weakness. Ingeniously, Marshall crafted a third way. The Court held that Adams's appointment of Marbury was valid, that Madison should have delivered Marbury's commission, but that Marbury had no legal remedy because the Court's authority to issue writs of *mandamus* was unconstitutional because this power was outside the authority granted to it by the Constitution. Marshall turned a no-win situation into one of the most masterful judicial power-plays of all time. By proclaiming that "[it] is emphatically the province and duty of the judicial department to say what the law is," Marshall's opinion in *Marbury* ensured the Supreme Court's co-equal status in relation to the Congress and President. In addition, the landmark decision confirmed the U.S. Constitution as the supreme law of the land.

McCulloch v. Maryland (1819) arose from the state of Maryland's attempts to impede the business of the Second Bank of the United States by placing a tax on every note it issued. McCulloch, a Second Bank cashier, refused to pay the tax. Two significant constitutional questions resulted from the impasse. First, did Congress have the authority to establish/re-establish the Bank? Second, if Congress did possess this power, did the Maryland law unconstitutionally interfere with that power? Marshall concluded that, although Congress did not have the enumerated power to create a national bank, it, likewise, was not explicitly prohibited from such action. Further, he determined that, because Congress did have certain enumerated powers, such as to lay and collect taxes and raise armies, it would also need the means to complete these tasks. The law chartering the Second Bank was a "necessary and proper" one (granted in Article I, Section 19 of the Constitution), which would allow Congress to act on its enumerated powers. Thus, Marshall's opinion in *McCulloch* reaffirmed the Constitution as the supreme law of the land, thereby making state law subordinate. As such, the Second Bank was a legitimate federal institution immune from the state's sovereign powers (including taxation). In expanding Congress's implied power, Marshall also strengthened the authority of the national government.

> "He had a more profound impact on American life than any other judge in our history. He established the Supreme Court's independence as a co-equal branch of government, enunciated and defended the essential principles of the American Union, and taught his contemporaries and posterity alike how to read and understand the United States Constitution-a task that amounted to the completion of the Founding."
>
> – Matthew Franck

In another of Marshall's most momentous decisions, *Dartmouth College v. Woodward* (1819), the Supreme Court afforded private parties protection from state and legislative interference. This case arose, much like *Marbury v. Madison*, as a result of the political differences between the Federalists and Jeffersonian Republicans. In 1818 Jefferson's party governed New Hampshire. The newly elected governor and legislature, unhappy with the Federalist Trustees at Dartmouth College, attempted to oust them and remake the college into a university under state control. Marshall concluded that the college was a private institution. As such, he viewed the Charter of Dartmouth College as a contract between a private entity and the state. The Constitution's Contract Clause, therefore, protected this private entity from state interference. Marshall's ruling placed a significant limitation on states' authority to regulate and interfere with private corporations.

Gibbons v. Ogden (1824) completes the historic quartet of decisions penned by Marshall. The case arose as a result of New York's attempts to regulate steamboat travel on its waterways. Thomas Gibbons held a federal coasting license that allowed him to travel between New Jersey and New York. Aaron Ogden held the state-required license. Gibbons contended that he was not required to pay any fees to New York because the federal license trumped any state license. Marshall implemented the Constitution's Supremacy Clause and concluded that Congress had the exclusive right to control interstate and foreign commerce. Once again, Marshall's jurisprudence served to strengthen the federal government's power.

Justice Benjamin Cardozo, who served briefly but brilliantly on the Supreme Court in the 1930s, wrote, "Marshall gave to the Constitution of the United States the impress of his own mind; and the form of our constitutional law is what it is, because he molded it while it was still plastic and malleable in the fire of his own intense convictions." "Those organ tones of his," he wrote elsewhere, "were meant to fill cathedrals." The Marshall Court led the federal government and gave it the means to develop and work. Lord Bryce, close student of American democracy and Britain's ambassador to the United States from 1907 to 1913, spoke of Marshall's decisions as "never having been surpassed and rarely equaled by the most famous jurists of modern Europe or of ancient Rome." When "The Great Chief Justice" died in 1835, his death hastened by a stage coach accident he suffered while riding judicial circuit, one newspaper eulogized, "Next to [George] Washington, only, did he possess the reverence and the homage of the heart of the American people."

MAIN CONTRIBUTIONS OF JOHN MARSHALL

Marshall bolstered the power of the U.S. Supreme Court, particularly by establishing the power of judicial review, and made it a co-equal branch of the federal government.

Marshall broadly interpreted Congress's implied power and declared it supreme over state authority. His interpretation that Congress's interstate commerce power is plenary set the stage for the national government's economic hegemony.

As the fourth Chief Justice of the United States, from 1801-1835, Marshall established the model of leadership for his successors on the nation's highest tribunal.

From the Pen of John Marshall

"That the people have an original right to establish, for their future government, such principles as, in their opinion shall most conduce to their own happiness, is the basis on which the whole American fabric has been erected. The exercise of this original right is a very great exertion; nor can it, nor ought it, to be frequently repeated. The principles, therefore, so established, are deemed fundamental. And as the authority from which they proceed, is supreme, and can seldom act, they are designed to be permanent.

This original and supreme will organizes the government, and assigns, to different departments, their respective powers. It may either stop here; or establish certain limits not to be transcended by those departments.

The government of the United States is of the latter description. The powers of the legislature are defined, and limited; and that those limits may not be mistaken, or forgotten, the constitution is written. To what purpose are powers limited, and to what purpose is the limitation committed to writing, if these limits may, at any time, be passed by those intended to be restrained? The distinction, between a government with limited and unlimited powers, is abolished, if those limits do not confine the persons on whom they are imposed, and if acts prohibited and acts allowed, are of equal obligation. It is a proposition too plain to be contested, that the constitution controls any legislative act repugnant to it; or, that the legislature may alter the constitution by an ordinary act.

Between these alternatives there is no middle ground. The constitution is either superior, paramount law, unchangeable by ordinary means, or it is on a level with ordinary legislative acts, and, like other acts, is alterable when the legislature shall please to alter it.

If the former part of the alternative be true, then a legislative act contrary to the constitution is not law: if the latter part be true, then written constitutions are absurd attempts, on the part of the people, to limit a power, in its own nature illimitable.

Certainly all those who have framed written constitutions contemplate them as forming the fundamental and paramount law of the nation, and consequently the theory of every such government must be, that an act of the legislature, repugnant to the constitution, is void.

This theory is essentially attached to a written constitution, and is, consequently to be considered by this court, as one of the fundamental principles of our society. It is not therefore to be lost sight of in the future consideration of this subject. . . .

It is emphatically the province and duty of the judicial department to say what the law is. Those who apply the rule to particular cases, must of necessity expound and interpret that rule. If two laws conflict with each other, the courts must decide on the operation of each."

–John Marshall, *Marbury v. Madison* (1803)

RECOMMENDED READING

Johnson, Herbert A. "John Marshall, 1801-1835." In Clare Cushman, ed. *The Supreme Court Justices: Illustrated Biographies, 1789-1993* (Washington: Congressional Quarterly, 1993).

Newmyer, R. Kent. *John Marshall and the Heroic Age of the Supreme Court* (Baton Rouge: Louisiana State University, 2001).

Simon, James F. *What Kind of Nation: Thomas Jefferson, John Marshall, and the Epic Struggle to Create a United States* (New York: Simon & Schuster, 2002).

Smith, Jean Edward. *John Marshall: Definer of a Nation* (New York: Henry Holt, 1996).

"For WHO ARE A FREE PEOPLE? Not *those*, over whom government is reasonable and equitably exercised, but *those*, who live under a government so *constitutionally checked and controlled*, that proper provision is made against its being otherwise exercised."

–John Dickinson, Letter VII,
Letters from a Farmer in Pennsylvania.

"Let these *truths* be indelibly impressed on our minds–*that* we *cannot be* HAPPY, *without being* FREE–that we cannot be free, *without being secure in our property*–that *we* cannot be secure in our property*, if, without our consent, others may, as by right, take it away. . . .*"

–John Dickinson, Letter XII,
Letters from a Farmer in Pennsylvania.

"Experience must be our only guide. Reason may mislead us."

–John Dickinson, Speech at the Constitutional Convention,
August 13, 1787.

JOHN DICKINSON
(1732-1808)

HOWARD L. LUBERT

When on July 2, 1776, John Dickinson abstained from the congressional vote on independence from Great Britain, he was not unaware of the effect his decision would have on his reputation. "My conduct this day I expect will give the finishing blow to my once too great, and, my integrity considered, now too diminished popularity ." Yet Dickinson's diminished fame does not accurately reflect the important role he played in America's Founding. Rightly dubbed the "Penman of the Revolution," no one played a more significant political role during the imperial crisis with Great Britain (1764-1776). More, he remained politically relevant after independence, helping to frame the Articles of Confederation, playing a notable role at the 1787 Constitutional Convention, and writing well-received essays in favor of the Constitution drafted by that convention.

Dickinson was born in Talbot County, Maryland, in November 1732. When he was eight years old his family moved, settling near Dover, Delaware. After being privately tutored, in 1750 Dickinson began to study law under John Moland in Philadelphia. He completed his legal studies in London at Middle Temple, one of England's four great "Inns of Court." He returned to Philadelphia in 1757, where he began a successful law practice. He soon entered politics, serving in the Delaware and Pennsylvania assemblies (1760-1765) where, according to a fellow assemblyman, Dickinson "greatly distinguished himself . . . as an orator."

Dickinson's first significant public act was to argue in May of 1764 against a proposal to ask King George III to replace Pennsylvania's proprietary government with a royal government. The plan, sponsored in part by Benjamin Franklin, a leader of the Popular or Quaker Party, sought to limit the broad political power of the colony's proprietors (the Penn family) and to subject their lands to the same taxes paid by the rest of the colony's residents. Dickinson found the Penn family's claim of exemption from taxes "fundamentally unjust" and "contradictory to the maxims of equity; and the spirit of liberty." But when Franklin, who had long desired to see the Proprietary government replaced, urged the assembly to ask for a revocation of the colony's charter, Dickinson broke with him. While Dickinson was not an advocate of the proprietary government, he questioned the "fatal speed" with which the assembly was moving. Further, he challenged the assumption that replacing the current government with a royal one could be accomplished without threatening crucial privileges–including religious liberty, the "best and greatest of all rights"–which the colony enjoyed under its 1701 Charter of Privileges. The summer and fall of 1764 were marked by a bitter newspaper war between Dickinson, on the one hand, and leaders of the Popular party, principally Joseph Galloway, on the other. When elections were held on October 1, Dickinson was reelected and Franklin and Galloway were defeated. However, the Popular party still controlled the assembly, and as that body moved forward with its plan to ask the King for a change of government, Dickinson decided that he would not seek reelection in October 1765.

Dickinson remained active in politics, taking the lead in formulating the colonial response to Parliament's passage of the Stamp Act (1765). In the process, he earned a reputation throughout the colonies as a Patriot as well as a thoughtful and articulate spokesman for the colonists' cause. The Pennsylvania assembly selected Dickinson as a delegate to the Stamp Act Congress in New York (October 1765) where he was the main author of the Congress's resolutions against the Act. In November he published *The Late Regulations respecting the British Colonies Considered*, which was printed in London the following year. *The Late Regulations* contended that the Stamp Act would hurt the prosperity of Great Britain and her colonies and, according to one London critic, was "highly esteemed" by the British public and "gained for the author much reputation." In other essays he wrote at the time, including *Friends and Countrymen* (1765) and the *Address to the Committee of Correspondence in Barbados* (1766), Dickinson defended the rights of the colonists and sketched out a constitutional argument about the nature of the Empire and the corresponding limits to Parliament's authority.

"Dickinson was one of the most admired and respected statesman and writers of his time in the colonies and early American Republic. . . His influence and eloquence are the best arguments against the rationalist Enlightenment view of the American Founding."
- E. Christian Kopff

Parliament's repeal of the Stamp Act in 1766 momentarily returned the colonies to a state of normalcy, but its passage of the Townshend Acts in June 1767, along with the Restraining Act suspending the New York legislature, rekindled Dickinson's fear that colonial liberties were increasingly in danger. Determined to sound the alarm, he adopted the persona of a common Pennsylvania farmer and began to write *Letters from a Farmer in Pennsylvania, To the Inhabitants of the British Colonies.* The first of these essays was published on December 2, 1767, and he continued to write one "letter" a week for twelve weeks. Although they were published under a pseudonym, Dickinson's authorship became public knowledge in May, 1768. The letters' importance was recognized immediately. Two days after publication of the first essay in the *Pennsylvania Chronicle and Universal Advisor*, it was reprinted in two other state newspapers. Ultimately, nineteen of the colonies' twenty-three newspapers printed all twelve of the *Farmer's Letters.* In March 1768, the first pamphlet version of the *Letters* was published, constituting one of seven separate editions that would be printed in the colonies in 1768 and 1769. Those years also saw publication of editions in London and Dublin and a French translation in Paris. In addition to his essays, Dickinson wrote a popular Patriotic anthem, "The Liberty Song," which was published in the *Boston Gazette* in July 1768 and later that year appeared in the *Boston Chronicle.* It was in this song that Dickinson coined the phrase, "By uniting we stand, by dividing we fall," a rallying cry that was most recently used after the attacks of September 11, 2001.

It is difficult to overstate the influence of Dickinson's *Farmer's Letters.* Until Thomas Paine published *Common Sense* in early 1776, no colonial publication received more praise or was more widely read than these essays. As Milton Flower noted in his biography of Dickinson, "Until the year of Independence, John Dickinson, apart from Benjamin Franklin, was probably the American known to more colonists than any other. Indeed, between the years of the Stamp Act crisis and the convening of the Second Continental Congress (1765-

1775), Dickinson was widely recognized as the chief spokesman for American rights and liberty." Public praise flowed in all forms. The College of New Jersey (Princeton) gave him an honorary degree in 1769. Paul Revere engraved a portrait plate of Dickinson for a 1772 Almanac. Patience Wright, the wax sculptor, added Dickinson's likeness to her collection. And in 1783, Dickinson College in Pennsylvania was chartered in his honor.

In response to Parliament's Tea Act of 1773, Dickinson again took up the pen to urge Americans to resist an unjust law. In July 1774, after the Boston Tea Party the previous December and the subsequent passage by Parliament of the harsh Boston Port Act, Dickinson drafted for the Provincial Convention of Pennsylvania a set of resolutions against the Act, along with a long statement explaining why Parliament's actions were unconstitutional. That long statement was published separately as *An Essay on the Constitutional Power of Great Britain* (1774). Then, as a delegate to the first Continental Congress, Dickinson drafted Congress's *Address to the Inhabitants of Quebec* and the *Petition to the King*.

When the Second Continental Congress convened in May 1775, Dickinson was again among the delegates. He penned drafts of Congress's "Olive Branch" petition and the *Declaration of the Causes and Necessity of Taking up Arms*. He also chaired the committee charged with drafting articles of union and produced the first working draft of those articles. But after the battles of Lexington and Concord in April 1775, Dickinson's desire for reconciliation with Great Britain was less and less politically tenable. In Congress, the forces promoting independence grew dominant, particularly after Thomas Paine published *Common Sense* in January 1776. He argued before

Congress on July 1 that it was premature to declare independence, but he persuaded few delegates. When the initial vote was taken, nine states voted for independence, with Delaware divided, New York abstaining, and South Carolina and Pennsylvania voting no. Hoping for unanimity, Congress delayed the official vote until the next day. With Caesar Rodney, after an all-night journey from Dover, breaking the tie for Delaware and South Carolina switching its vote, only Pennsylvania and New York remained. The New York delegates were not authorized to vote on the question and again abstained. Pennsylvania potentially stood in the way of a unanimous vote for independence, but John Dickinson and Robert Morris abstained from voting, thus allowing the state's delegation to vote in favor of independence. Congress was thereby able to claim that the Declaration had passed without any colony dissenting.

> "Dickinson's thought bears the deep impression of the Western tradition of liberal learning."
>
> –Richard Gamble

As suggested earlier, Dickinson's refusal to vote for independence has hurt his reputation. His role in the Founding Era has often been minimized and even distorted. At least one website erroneously claims that he was a Loyalist, and numerous scholars, following the unfair characterization of him painted by John Adams, have labeled him conservative, cautious, and timid. It is important to remember, however, that for a decade Dickinson urged resistance to the first signs of British tyranny. While he preferred to maintain colonial rights within the existing Empire, he also believed that preserving those rights took priority over maintaining the Empire. His cautiousness was prudential, not ideological or temperamental; he thought the vote on independence ill-timed, coming before a new national government had been constructed and before any foreign aid had been secured. Until that vote, he had been the leading penman in defense of the colonists' rights.

After America's declaration of independence, Dickinson left Congress and took up his position as colonel of the First Philadelphia Battalion of Associators, a volunteer battalion that headed north to meet an expected British invasion of New York. In 1777, Dickinson, who at that time owned 37 slaves and was Delaware's largest slaveholder, freed his slaves. Why he decided at this moment to manumit them is not entirely clear; however, pressure from the surrounding Quaker community (Dickinson was a Quaker), along with the pervasive talk of liberty and rights that filled the air, undoubtedly played a role in his decision. He returned to Congress in 1779, and in 1781 was elected president of Delaware. In October 1782, he was elected to the Supreme Executive Council of Pennsylvania (at the time Pennsylvania had a multi-member executive), and for a brief period he served as executive for both states. In 1786, Dickinson attended and was made President of the Annapolis Convention, a meeting called to "remedy defects of the federal government." Because only five states sent delegates, the convention could do little other than call for another one to be held in Philadelphia the following May.

Delaware appointed Dickinson to represent the state in the Federal Constitutional Convention of 1787. Although his attendance was interrupted by ill health, he was an active participant, and he was instrumental in laying the seed for what would later become known as the "Great" or "Connecticut" compromise, which resolved the dispute between large and small states over representation in Congress. He also joined debates regarding the executive branch. After the Convention adjourned, Dickinson wrote nine essays urging the Constitution's ratification. These *Letters of Fabius*, which appeared in the *Delaware Gazette* beginning in early 1788 and in pamphlet form that April, were praised by Washington and other Federalists.

> "The "penman" of the Revolution."
>
> —Scott Gerber

Dickinson began a slow process of retiring from public life after the Constitution was ratified. In 1791, he served as President of the Delaware Convention called to revise that state's constitution and was one of the chief authors of the new constitution. His last notable public acts were to publish in 1797–again under the pseudonym "Fabius"–a series of fifteen letters sympathetic to France in response to what became known as the XYZ affair, and then in 1803 wrote *An Address on the Past, Present, and Eventual Relations of the United States to France* (signed "Anticipation"), which in light of Napoleon's march through Europe took a more sober view of those relations. Dickinson's primary occupation after 1788, however, was to live quietly with his wife Mary and two daughters in Wilmington, Delaware. In 1801, he published a two-volume collection of his writings. He died on February 14, 1808, at his Wilmington home. Upon news of his passing, Congress resolved to wear black crêpe armbands in his honor and public praise poured forth. As President Jefferson remarked, "Among the first of the advocates of the rights of his country when assailed by Great Britain, he continued to the last the orthodox advocate of the true principles of our new government."

MAIN CONTRIBUTIONS
OF JOHN DICKINSON

Dickinson was the author of the important series of essays, *Letters from a Farmer in Pennsylvania* (1767-1768). He has been called "Penman of the Revolution."

Dickinson was a member of the Constitutional Convention of 1787 and author of the significant Federalist essays, *The Letters of Fabius*, in 1788, on the Federal Constitution.

Dickinson was a delegate to the Stamp Act Congress (1765), the First and Second Continental Congresses (1774-75), the Annapolis Convention (1786), and the Constitutional Convention (1787).

From the Pen of John Dickinson

"It is true that *impositions for raising a revenue*, may be hereafter called *regulations of trade* : But names will not change the nature of things. Indeed we ought firmly to believe, what is an undoubted truth, confirmed by the unhappy experience of many states heretofore free, that UNLESS THE MOST WATCHFUL ATTENTION BE EXERTED, A NEW SERVITUDE MAY BE

SLIPPED UPON US, UNDER THE SANCTION OF USUAL AND RESPECTABLE TERMS.

Thus the Caesars ruined the Roman liberty, under the titles of *tribunicial and dictatorial* authorities–old and venerable dignities, known in the most flourishing times of freedom. In imitation of the same policy, James II when he *meant* to establish popery, *talked* of liberty of conscience, the most sacred of all liberties; and had thereby almost deceived the Dissenters into destruction.

All artful rulers, who strive to extend their power beyond its just limits, endeavor to give to their attempts as much semblance of legality as possible. Those who succeed them may venture to go a little further; for each new encroachment will be strengthened by a former. 'That which is now supported by examples, growing old, will become an example itself' and thus support fresh usurpations.

A FREE people therefore can never be too quick in observing, nor too firm in opposing the beginnings of *alteration* either in *form* or *reality*, respecting institutions formed for their security. The first kind of alteration leads to the last: Yet, on the other hand, nothing is more certain, than that the *forms* of liberty may be retained, when the *substance* is gone. In government, as well as in religion, 'The *letter* killeth, but the *spirit* giveth life'."

–John Dickinson, Letter VI, *Letters from a Farmer in Pennsylvania*

RECOMMENDED READING

Milton Flower, *John Dickinson, Conservative Revolutionary* (Charlottesville: University Press of Virginia, 1983).

Forrest McDonald and Ellen S. McDonald, "John Dickinson, Founding Father," *Delaware History* 23 (1988): 24-38.

Jane E. Calvert, "Liberty without Tumult: Understanding the Politics of John Dickinson," *The Pennsylvania Magazine of History and Biography* 131 (July 2007): 233-262.

"[I]n America THE LAW IS KING."

–Thomas Paine, *Common Sense*, 1776

"These are the times that try men's souls. The summer soldier and the sunshine Patriot will, in this crisis, shrink from the service of his country; but he that stands [by] it NOW, deserves the love and thanks of man and woman. Tyranny, like hell, is not easily conquered; yet we have this consolation with us, that the harder the conflict, the more glorious the triumph."

–Thomas Paine, *The American Crisis,* No. 1, December 23, 1776

"My motive and object in all my political works, beginning with Common Sense, . . . have been to rescue man from tyranny and false systems and false principles of government, and enable him to be free, and establish government for himself."

–Thomas Paine to John Inskeep, *Philadelphia Commercial Advertiser,* February 10, 1806

THOMAS PAINE
(1737-1809)

DAVID VOELKER

Thomas Paine was not the only Founder to be born outside of the thirteen colonies, but for a latecomer to America he made an astonishing impact on the revolutionary struggle. Paine arrived in Philadelphia in late 1774 at the age of thirty-seven, after suffering a variety of personal setbacks. He briefly edited a successful magazine in 1775 and then applied his talents to promoting the Revolutionary cause. His pamphlet Common Sense, *published in early 1776, championed independence and helped turn the tide of public opinion in that direction. Paine's fame in America crested during the Revolution, when he wrote a series of pamphlets to inspire the Patriot cause. His subsequent involvement in the French Revolution and vehement attacks on Christianity, however, damaged his reputation. Nevertheless, Paine deserves recognition as a Founder, not only because his pro-revolutionary rhetoric inspired Patriots throughout the American War for Independence but also because he helped ordinary colonists envision a prosperous American future under republican government.*

Thomas Paine was born into a family of modest means in Thetford, England, a town about eighty miles from London, on January 29, 1737. Paine's mother belonged to the Church of England and saw her son baptized into this established church of the realm, but Paine was also influenced by his father's membership in the more egalitarian Society of Friends (or Quakers), a dissenting group that was merely tolerated. As a young man, Paine split the difference between his parents' churches and affiliated with Methodists, who represented a popular and evangelical offshoot of the Church of England. In the late 1750s, Paine even sometimes exhorted, or preached informally, for the Methodists.

Despite his religious upbringing, Paine eventually fell under the influence of Newtonian science, which imagined the universe to be an orderly and mechanistic–rather than a miraculous–place. By the time that he arrived in America in late 1774, Paine had already become quite impious, questioning the legitimacy of the Bible, the reality of miracles, and even the divinity of Jesus. He mostly kept his critiques of Christianity to himself at that time however, and when he argued for the cause of independence, he drew heavily on the Bible to enrich his rhetoric. It was only in 1794, when he published a pamphlet entitled, *The Age of Reason,* that Paine unleashed a vehement attack on Christianity, thus severely damaging his reputation in America. Paine's avid support of the French Revolution, which turned murderous and indeed nearly took Paine's own life, also took its toll on his popularity in America, as did his public criticism of George Washington in 1796 for endorsing the pro-British Jay Treaty.

After Paine returned to America in 1802, he suffered the humiliation of being denied the right to vote, and many of his former friends and colleagues refused to associate with him. Because he returned in the midst of a heated political battle between Republicans and Federalists, a battle in which Federalists accused the Republican leader Thomas Jefferson of being anti-Christian and Francophile, Paine became something of a *persona non grata.* Although Paine and his pro-republican, anti-clerical writings continued to be quite influential among social critics, religious upstarts, and populist reformers, he was hardly welcomed into the pantheon of the "Founding Fathers." Paine, however, deserves recognition as a Founder, not only because his pro-revolutionary rhetoric inspired Patriots throughout the American War for Independence, but also because he articulated what historian Harvey Kaye (*Thomas Paine and the Promise of America)* has called "the promise of America." Paine helped sell the revolution to ordinary, free colonists by envisioning a prosperous American future under republican government.

> "He became the great voice of revolution with publication of *Common Sense* in 1776 and rallied the Patriot cause with the series of sixteen pamphlets under the title *The American Crisis* until the end of the Revolution in 1783."
>
> —Ellis Sandoz

The first thirty-seven years of Paine's life were marred by misfortune and frustration, but they also allowed Paine to begin developing talents that would serve him well later in his life. As a child, Paine attended grammar school for several years, but he spent his teenage years as an apprentice in his father's staymaking shop, where he learned to make stays for women's corsets from baleen, or whalebone. After a brief stint at sea as a privateer during the Seven Years War, Paine settled down to work as a staymaker and married Mary Lambert, but she died within a year. Paine then worked as an excise tax officer for about three years, but was fired for alleged misconduct. After working again as a staymaker and then briefly as a teacher, he regained employment as a tax officer, married a woman named Elizabeth Ollive, and became active in a political debating group revealingly known as the "Headstrong Club." During the winter of 1772–73, he wrote and published his first pamphlet, in which he campaigned for higher pay for his fellow tax collectors. Because he neglected his own professional duties while lobbying in London on behalf of the excisemen, he lost his job, and his small business back home also failed. Meanwhile, his second marriage collapsed. While still in London, Paine had the fortunate opportunity of meeting Benjamin Franklin, who wrote a letter of introduction for Paine and suggested that he seek his fortune across the Atlantic. Having little to lose, Paine booked passage to Philadelphia in late 1774.

Without the aid of Franklin's letter, addressed to his son-in-law in Philadelphia, Paine may well have perished. Upon his arrival in Philadelphia, Paine was so ill that he had to be carried from the ship on a litter. His fortune, however, soon improved. After he recovered, he was browsing a bookstore in Philadelphia and struck up a conversation with the store's owner, Robert Aitken. Aitken happened to be seeking an editor for *The Pennsylvania Magazine*, which he and John Witherspoon were planning to publish. Paine's program of educating himself through reading, attending lectures, and participating in debates and coffeehouse discussions paid off. He was able to show Aitken some of his writing samples and landed the job as editor.

Paine thus immersed himself in the exciting intellectual and political currents of Philadelphia in 1775. *The Philadelphia Magazine* quickly gained wide readership. He soon joined the first antislavery society in America, which was inspired in part by an antislavery essay that he had published anonymously. Paine's new home of Philadelphia played an important role in the growing imperial crisis. Just before his arrival, the First Continental Congress, with delegates from twelve colonies, had met in the city. Protesting taxation without representation, the perversion of the imperial judicial system, and the treatment of Boston and Massachusetts in the wake of the Boston Tea Party, the Congress declared their rights according to their understanding of the English constitution and resolved to pressure Parliament through a non-importation, non-consumption, and non-exportation agreement. Tensions between the colonies and imperial government escalated into violence the following spring. On April 19, 1775, fighting broke out between the "minutemen" of Lexington and Concord (in Massachusetts), and the British soldiers who had marched out of Boston in search of colonial stockpiles of arms and ammunition. By May 10, the Second Continental Congress convened in Philadelphia, and a month later, the Congress created a Continental Army to be led by George Washington.

> "For his peerless role as the pamphleteer of the American Revolution, in the course of which he transformed and extended the language of American politics, Paine deserves inclusion."
>
> —R. B. Bernstein

Although Paine did not yet jump directly into the political fray, the February 1775 issue of his magazine included an essay critical of the colonial consumption of British tea. By July, the magazine published two allegorical essays that championed the right of the colonists to defend their liberty and property from British aggression. More strikingly, the magazine reprinted the Second Continental Congress's strident "Declaration . . . Setting Forth the Causes and Necessity of their Taking

Up Arms," which reached a powerful conclusion:

> "In our own native land, in defence of the freedom
> that is our birthright, and which we ever enjoyed
> till the late violation of it–for the protection of our
> property, acquired solely by the honest industry
> of our fore-fathers and ourselves, against violence
> actually offered, we have taken up arms. We shall lay
> them down when hostilities shall cease on the part of
> the aggressors, and all danger of their being renewed
> shall be removed, and not before."

Paine's magazine thus signaled that it came down squarely on the side
of the aggrieved colonists.

By the fall of 1775, Paine had concluded that the American colonies
needed to unite behind the cause of independence. He had also
reached the end of his partnership with Aitken and Witherspoon; he
resigned his editorship because of disagreements over his salary. His
break from the magazine, however, freed him to compose a pamphlet
in support of independence–a project that he had been discussing with
Philadelphia physician Benjamin Rush (another neglected Founder).

Published anonymously in January 1776, Paine's *Common Sense*
became the most widely read pamphlet in eighteenth century America
(by far). Hundreds of thousands of colonists either read the pamphlet
themselves or heard it read aloud and discussed. Drawing on history,
Biblical examples, and what he called "common sense," Paine took a
novel approach to arguing for independence. Most of his fellow Patriots
had long admired the English constitution. Indeed, the various protest

documents issued by the colonists appealed to the English constitution–which was a political and legal tradition rather than a single written document–as the source of their liberties. Paine, by contrast, directly attacked the constitution by condemning the monarchy and aristocracy. He even attacked the structure of English society itself as fundamentally dysfunctional. Furthermore, he pointed out the absurdity of an island governing the continent of North America indefinitely. He also dramatized the importance of the Patriot cause in memorable language: "The sun never shined on a cause of greater worth. 'Tis not the affair of a city, a country, a province, or a kingdom, but of a continent . . . . 'Tis not the concern of a day, a year, or an age; posterity are virtually involved in the contest, and will be more or less affected, even until the end of time. Now is the seed time of continental union, faith, and honor."

Common Sense went even further to make the case for independence. First, Paine addressed the pamphlet to ordinary Americans, making it clear that they had a stake in the future status of their provinces. He accomplished this end in part by writing in accessible and vivid prose, with frequent allusions to the well-known literature of the Protestant Bible. Paine also used his political imagination to project an image of a democratic republic. Visualizing a primordial political assembly, for example, Paine wrote: "Some convenient tree will afford them a State-House, under the branches of which, the whole colony may assemble to deliberate on public matters." He also made suggestions about the future government of the "United Colonies." Here, he boldly recommended that the colonies hold a conference to frame a "CONTINENTAL CHARTER," which amounted to nothing less than a written constitution. In sum, Paine sketched a powerful image of a republican society, a society where all citizens would be equal, where the law would be king, and where Americans of all origins and faiths could pursue prosperity in peace.

Historians agree that Paine's *Common Sense* helped convince colonists that the time had indeed come for declaring independence, but it is also worth noting Paine's contribution to the concept of American exceptionalism–the belief that America offered unique opportunities for freedom and prosperity and that the American people had a special duty to strive to fulfill this destiny. Near the conclusion of *Common Sense,* for example, Paine declared: "We have it in our power to begin the world over again. A situation, similar to the present, hath not happened since the days of Noah until now. The birthday of a new world is at hand, and a race of men, perhaps as numerous as all Europe contains, are to receive their portion of freedom from the event of a few months." Although Paine later repudiated any belief in special providence (God's direct intervention in human affairs), his *American Crisis* pamphlet series brimmed with references to God favoring the Patriot cause. At the close of the January 13, 1777, *Crisis,* for instance, Paine predicted: "Our independence, with God's blessing, we will maintain against all the world." In all of his revolutionary writings, Paine conveyed the notion that God supported American liberation, and "Americans"–a label that Paine promoted–had an obligation to seize the opportunity. In *The Last Crisis* of April 19, 1783, Paine reiterated the Revolution's significance: "To see it in our power to make a world happy–to teach mankind the art of being so–to exhibit on the theatre of the universe a character hitherto unknown–and to have, as it were, a new creation entrusted to our hands, are honors that command reflection, and can neither be too highly estimated, nor too gratefully received." With this sort of rhetoric, Paine contributed to Americans' sense that their especially blessed nation had a unique mission to promote liberty.

Paine gave his most important service to the Revolutionary cause as a pamphleteer, with all royalties for his publications going to support the war effort, but he also filled various official posts during the war. In the summer of 1776, Paine enlisted in a militia unit as secretary to General Daniel Roberdea; when that term ended in the fall of 1776, he enlisted in the Continental Army, where he served as an aide to General Nathaniel Greene. Between 1777 and 1779, Paine worked as secretary to the Continental Congress's Committee on Foreign Affairs. Meanwhile, he promoted the unusually democratic constitution of Pennsylvania, whose framers had been deeply influenced by the constitutional plan that he had laid out in *Common Sense.* From 1779 to 1781, he served as the clerk for Pennsylvania's legislative assembly. In 1781, he traveled to France to solicit wartime assistance, and he even participated in combat during the journey. Unfortunately for his livelihood, Paine also made a number of political enemies by (legitimately) attacking Silas Deane, an American agent to France, with charges of corruption. As the Revolution came to a close, Paine found himself unemployed, but by 1785 he had garnered modest grants of money and land from Pennsylvania, New York, and Congress.

After the war, Paine continued to write on political issues important to establishing national unity, but he turned his attention to another type of project, namely promoting his design for an iron bridge capable of spanning long distances. Although he pursued this project for several years and made significant engineering advancements, his quests to secure funding in the U.S., Britain, and France all fell short, and he never fully implemented his design.

By 1789, international developments redirected Paine's energies back toward revolutionary politics. That summer, a popular uprising in France led to the overthrow of the feudal order and the establishment, initially, of a constitutional monarchy. When British conservative Edmund Burke decried the revolutionary disorder in a widely read treatise of 1790, Paine responded with a two-part pamphlet entitled *Rights of Man* (1791–92). For an eighteenth-century political pamphlet, the popularity of *Rights of Man* was second only to *Common Sense,* but its influence spread even broader, as it was read not only in the U.S. and Britain, but also in France and elsewhere in Europe. *Rights of Man* reaffirmed and elaborated upon the political principles that Paine had first sketched out in *Common Sense,* especially the "equality of man" and the right to self government. Because the tract threatened monarchical authority, Paine was convicted in Britain *in absentia* of seditious libel; his writings were banned in Britain, and he was effectively exiled.

Paine narrowly escaped arrest in Britain in September 1792 by fleeing to France, where he had been awarded honorary citizenship and a seat in the National Convention. He did not speak fluent French, but he was appointed to a committee charged with drafting a constitution. Despite his prominent position, Paine soon found himself in serious jeopardy. As two factions struggled for control over the revolutionary government, Paine sided with the moderate Girondins by (unsuccessfully) opposing the execution of King Louis XVI. When the radical Jacobins, led by Maximilian Robespierre, seized power in 1793, they began arresting and executing their political enemies. Along with other foreigners, Paine found himself ejected from the Convention in December 1793 and imprisoned. While in prison for nearly a year, Paine suffered from ill health and narrowly escaped execution. Thanks to the advocacy of James Monroe, the American ambassador to France, Paine was released from prison in late 1794 and was restored to his position in the Convention, where he continued to serve through the following year.

Just before he was imprisoned, Paine completed the manuscript for the first part of *The Age of Reason: Being an Investigation of True and of Fabulous Theology,* which was published in the U.S. in two parts in 1794 and 1795 and was also translated into French. Paine wrote *The Age of Reason* in part to respond to the political emergency that threatened his own life. As he later explained in a public letter to Samuel Adams (who was deeply offended by the book), "[m]y friends were falling as fast as the guillotine could cut their heads off," and "the people of France were running headlong into Atheism." Although most Americans perceived *The Age of Reason* primarily as a scurrilous attack on Christianity in particular and revealed religion in general, Paine also wrote to promote a deistic morality that he believed would prevent atrocities like the Jacobin Terror.

Nevertheless, he devoted most of the work to condemning Christianity. "The Christian theory," he wrote, "is little else than the idolatry of the ancient mythologists, accommodated to the purposes of power and revenue." Paine expressed equally harsh views of the Bible: "When I see throughout the greatest part of this book, scarcely any thing but a history of the grossest vices, and a collection of the most paltry and contemptible tales, I cannot dishonour my Creator by calling it by his name." As for Jesus, Paine believed that "He was a virtuous and an amiable man" who preached a "benevolent" morality that "has not been exceeded by any." Not surprisingly, however, Paine rejected and condemned the supernatural aura surrounding Jesus, whom he considered to be merely human. Paine rejected the Christian virtue of loving one's enemy, as he found it impracticable, but he suggested that the moral implications of the "book of Creation" were clear: "The Almighty lecturer, by displaying the principles of science in the structure of the universe, has invited man to study and to imitation. It is as if he had said to the inhabitants of this globe that we call ours, 'I have made an earth for man to dwell upon, and I have rendered the starry heavens visible, to teach him science and the arts. He can now provide for his own comfort, AND LEARN FROM MY MUNIFICENCE TO ALL, TO BE KIND TO EACH OTHER.'" Creation, according to Paine, enjoined humanity to follow the golden rule.

The Age of Reason went through an impressive twenty-one American reprints within a decade. But the denunciations came quickly as well. Within fifteen years, the book had been met with almost seventy responses in America and England. Several years later, in 1802, after Paine became disillusioned with Napoleon and left France for America, he found that his reputation there had been severely tarnished. To be sure, some of his old friends welcomed him heartily, as did substantial numbers of the Democratic-Republicans. He maintained friendships with Thomas Jefferson (who helped him return to America), James Monroe (who had helped secure his release from prison in France), and James Madison. Many of his associates from the revolutionary period, however, turned their backs on Paine. John Adams (who had long mistrusted Paine), Samuel Adams, Benjamin Rush, John Jay, Patrick Henry, and Elias Boudinot all reacted very negatively to Paine's attacks on Christianity.

Nevertheless, Paine was by no means forgotten after his death in 1809. On the contrary, as Harvey Kaye has argued in *Thomas Paine and the Promise of America*, Paine's writings inspired not only deists and other religious outsiders but also a wide variety of democratic reformers and freethinkers.

Paine's legacy lived on, as nineteenth century Americans continued to spread the influence of republican principles and to expand the nation that he helped create.

MAIN CONTRIBUTIONS
OF THOMAS PAINE

Paine's pamphlet *Common Sense* played a crucial role in persuading Americans that the time had come to declare independence from Britain. Crucially, the pamphlet envisioned a prosperous future for an egalitarian and self-governed America.

Paine's pamphlet series, *The American Crisis*, helped sustain Patriotism throughout the revolutionary war.

Paine's writings promoted a republican and democratic spirit that inspired generations of American activists and reformers.

From the Pen of Thomas Paine

"The cause of America is in a great measure the cause of all mankind. Many circumstances hath, and will arise, which are not local, but universal, and through which the principles of all Lovers of Mankind are affected, and in the Event of which, their Affections are interested. The laying of a Country desolate with Fire and Sword, declaring War against the natural rights of all Mankind, and extirpating the Defenders thereof from the Face of the Earth, is the Concern of every Man to whom Nature hath given the Power of feeling . . .

A government of our own is our natural right: And when a man seriously reflects on the precariousness of human affairs, he will become convinced, that it is infinitely wiser and safer, to form a constitution of our own in a cool deliberate manner, while we have it in our power, than to trust such an interesting event to time and chance.

O ye that love mankind! Ye that dare oppose, not only the tyranny, but the tyrant, stand forth! Every spot of the old world is overrun with oppression. Freedom hath been hunted round the globe. Asia, and Africa, have long expelled her. –Europe regards her like a stranger, and England hath given her warning to depart. O! receive the fugitive, and prepare in time an asylum for mankind."

–Thomas Paine, *Common Sense* (1776)

RECOMMENDED READING

Harvey Kaye, *Thomas Paine and the Promise of America* (New York: Hill and Wang, 2005).

John Keane, *Tom Paine: A Political Life* (New York: Grove Press, 2003).

The Thomas Paine Reader, Ed. Michael Foot and Isaac Kramnick. (New York: Penguin, 1987).

"I have but one lamp by which my feet are guided, and that is the lamp of experience. I know of no way of judging of the future but by the past."

–Patrick Henry, "Liberty or Death" speech, 1775

"This Constitution is said to have beautiful features; but when I come to examine these features, Sir, they appear to me horridly frightful: Among other deformities, it has an awful squinting; it squints towards monarchy."

–Patrick Henry, Speech at Virginia Ratifying Convention, 1788

PATRICK HENRY
(1736-1799)

THOMAS S. KIDD

Patrick Henry was one of the most influential Patriots who promoted resistance to British authority during the American Revolution. In 1765, as a freshman member of Virginia's colonial legislature, Henry introduced the Stamp Act Resolutions, and gave a fiery speech against King George III that elicited cries of treason from other legislators. Henry served in the First and Second Continental Congresses, but his most famous speech came at the Virginia Convention in March 1775, where he famously declared "Give me liberty or give me death!" The popular Henry led a militia to recover gunpowder seized by Virginia's royal governor in April 1775. Once independence was proclaimed, Henry served as Virginia's first governor from 1776-79, an office he held again from 1784-86. During the 1780s, Henry disagreed with his fellow revolutionary leaders James Madison and Thomas Jefferson over a number of issues, including the role of religion in Virginia society. While Madison successfully pushed through Jefferson's Bill for Establishing Religious Freedom in 1786, Henry advocated continued state support for Christian ministers. Henry also opposed Madison's new Federal Constitution in 1787-88, and Henry became one of America's leading Anti-Federalists. He eventually became supportive of the new federal government, and remained especially close with George Washington.

Patrick Henry was born on May 29, 1736, to John and Sarah

Henry of Hanover County, Virginia. Henry's family did not belong to the old Virginia aristocracy, but they were up-and-coming residents of central Virginia. Henry only briefly attended grammar school, and did not go to college. Nevertheless, he received significant training from his father in essential topics of the liberal arts, especially ancient and modern history.

Henry married his first wife Sarah in 1754, and twice as a young man he launched small stores that went bankrupt. He briefly worked as a barkeeper at his father-in-law's tavern, where he first met Thomas Jefferson in 1759. There had been little indication of Henry's coming rise to prominence when he finally acquired his law license in 1760.

One of the formative influences on Henry as a youth was the new evangelical faith emerging from the First Great Awakening that started in the 1740s. Virginia maintained state support for the Anglican church (Church of England), so the emotional preaching style of the upstart Presbyterians and Baptists was not welcomed by many Virginians. But Henry's mother came under the influence of the Hanover's famous Presbyterian pastor Samuel Davies, whose compelling sermons won her over. She reportedly took young Patrick to Davies' meetings in the 1740s, and Henry remembered Davies as the "greatest orator he ever heard." Although Henry remained an Anglican, he adapted the evangelical preaching style to his political speeches, with explosive results.

Religious issues also gave Henry his first opportunity to confront the problem of royal authority in America in a case that became known as the Parson's Cause. Virginia reduced Anglican priests' salaries under the Two Penny Act of 1758, but the British Privy Council, with approval from the king, overturned the law. Henry defended Louisa County, Virginia, in a lawsuit brought by one of the priests to recover lost salary. Henry turned the case into an attack on British power in the colonies, exclaiming that "a King, by annulling or disallowing Laws of this salutary Nature, from being the Father of his People, degenerates into a Tyrant, and forfeits all Right to his Subjects' Obedience." Having tapped into popular resentment against Britain, Henry convinced the jury to insult the priest further by awarding only one penny in damages.

> "Like many Americans over the course of the rest of American history he believed that our inalienable rights were best protected by strong and vigorous state and local governments."
> – Stephen B. Presser

Henry's growing popularity led to his election to the Virginia House of Burgesses, the colonial legislature, in 1765. His arrival in the House coincided with the coming of the Stamp Act Crisis, during which many Americans began to protest the imposition of taxes by Parliament. Henry immediately seized the spotlight by introducing resolutions against the Stamp Act, helping Americans articulate their belief that they should only be taxed by their own elected legislatures, not Parliament.

In his speech defending the resolutions, Henry again challenged not only Parliament's power, but most provocatively, the king's. A visitor to the House reported that Henry proclaimed that "in former times Tarquin and Jul[i]us had their Brutus, Charles had his Cromwell, and he did not doubt but some good American would stand up, in favour of his Country." The implication seemed clear–Henry was warning that King George III might be assassinated if he became tyrannical. Understandably, the speech drew a rebuke from the speaker, who declared that Henry had spoken treason. Henry backed down, but he had made his point. The resolutions electrified the colonies, giving a focal point to the growing resistance movement.

Henry moved in and out of the spotlight in the Revolutionary crisis, as he continued to spend a great deal of time on private business and legal affairs. But in 1774, as the tension between Britain and the colonies entered its most acute phase, Virginians chose him to serve along with George Washington and others in the First Continental Congress in Philadelphia. One of Henry's greatest moments in the Congress came when he proclaimed that "the distinctions between Virginians, Pennsylvanians, New Yorkers, and New Englanders, are no more. I am not a Virginian, but an American." Intercolonial cooperation was nearly unprecedented, but was badly needed in light of the coming struggle. Henry, with other radicals such as John and Samuel Adams, prevented the Congress from offering conciliatory measures, and helped steer America toward war.

Back in Virginia, Henry's support for defensive measures against Britain led him to give his most celebrated oration, the "Liberty or Death" speech. While some Virginians hesitated at the prospect of armed conflict, Henry demanded that the time for war had come: "We must fight! I repeat it, sir, we must fight! An appeal to arms and to the God of hosts, is all that is left us!. . .Is life so dear, or peace so sweet, as to be purchased at the price of chains and slavery? Forbid it, Almighty God!" With this, Henry lifted his arms and cried, "I know not what course others may take; but as for me, give me liberty, or give me death!" The exhilarated Virginia Convention adopted Henry's plan for defending itself against Britain.

Soon after the "Liberty or Death" speech, Virginia's royal governor, Lord Dunmore, decided to seize the colonists' gunpowder held at Williamsburg. Henry, becoming as much a military leader as a politician, led a volunteer militia company from Hanover County to re-take the gunpowder. Cooler heads prevailed, and Henry accepted a promise of compensation for the gunpowder from the governor's agents. The angry Dunmore still declared Henry an outlaw, however. Henry's persistent radicalism helped set the stage for Virginia, and America, to declare independence in 1776.

Henry was an obvious choice as Virginia's first governor, an office which he held from 1776-1779, and again from 1784-1786. In 1777, Henry married his second wife, Dorothea, following the death of his first wife Sarah in 1775. Altogether, Henry had seventeen children.

During the 1780s, Henry developed a bitter rivalry with his former Patriot brethren Thomas Jefferson and James Madison. Jefferson, working as an ambassador in Paris, became so disgusted with the feud that he once wrote Madison that they should pray for Henry to die. One of the sharpest points of contention between them was state support for religion in Virginia. Tax support for the Anglican Church had been suspended in 1776, but many Virginians, including Henry and George Washington, still believed that a moral society needed government support for religion. In 1784, Henry introduced a measure for a "general assessment" for religion, under which residents could designate the church to receive their taxes. But when Henry left the legislature to return to the governor's mansion, Madison seized the opportunity to defeat Henry's plan. A flood of petitions from non-Episcopal evangelicals opposed the general assessment. Riding the wave of popular sentiment, Madison managed to pass Jefferson's Bill for Establishing Religious Freedom in 1786. This act banned tax support for religion and prohibited legal penalties for unorthodox beliefs.

Henry also opposed Madison's new constitution for the United States, adopted at the Constitutional Convention in 1787. Henry became one of America's most influential Anti-Federalists, arguing that the proposed constitution threatened the states with unchecked national power. Henry's opposition to the Constitution may be difficult to understand today, but he represented a number of prominent Patriot leaders who had serious misgivings about the proposed new government. As legal historian Stephen B. Presser has noted, "Like many Americans over the course of the rest of American history, Henry believed that our inalienable rights were best protected by strong and vigorous state and local governments." He could not stomach the vast new powers afforded to the national government.

"Henry's powerful oratory was instrumental in marshalling Americans to the cause of independence in the early to mid-1770s. In the late 1780s, he emerged as leading anti-federalist, and his opposition to the proposed national constitution of 1787 was responsible, in part, for the debate over amendments to the Constitution, which resulted in the adoption of the U.S. Bill of Rights."

— Daniel L. Dreisbach

At the Virginia Ratifying Convention, Henry nearly convinced delegates to reject the Constitution, warning that it represented "a revolution as radical as that which separated us from Great Britain.

. .The rights of conscience, trial by jury, liberty of the press, all your immunities and franchises, all pretensions to human rights and privileges, are rendered insecure, if not lost, by this change." The adoption of the Bill of Rights by the first Congress helped alleviate some of these fears, and Henry quickly reconciled with the new government.

By the 1790s, Henry had seemingly switched roles with Jefferson and Madison, as Henry became affiliated with Washington's Federalist party, and at times defended stronger national power. After declining several federal positions, including Secretary of State in 1795, Henry was again elected to Virginia's legislature in 1799. He died that year before taking office.

Henry was greatly admired by other Revolutionary leaders, primarily for his courage and oratorical brilliance. Silas Deane of Connecticut wrote that Henry was the "compleatest speaker I ever heard. . .but in a letter I can give you no idea of the music of his voice, or the highwrought yet natural elegance of his style and manner." George Mason of Virginia wrote that Henry was "by far the most powerful speaker I ever heard. Every word he says not only engages but commands the attention; and your passions are no longer your own when he addresses them. But his eloquence is the smallest part of his merit. He is in my opinion the first man upon this continent, as well in abilities as public virtues, and had he lived in Rome about the time of the first Punic War, when the Roman people had arrived at their meridian glory, and their virtue not tarnished, Mr. Henry's talents must have put him at the head of that glorious commonwealth."

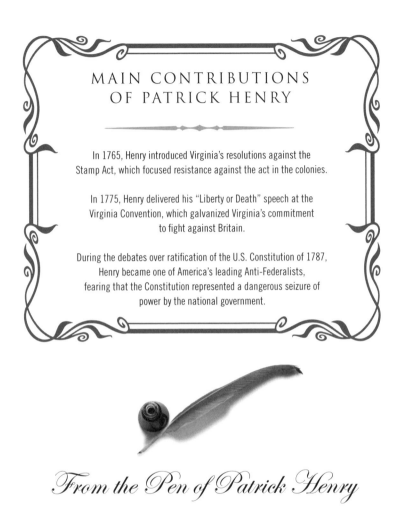

MAIN CONTRIBUTIONS OF PATRICK HENRY

In 1765, Henry introduced Virginia's resolutions against the Stamp Act, which focused resistance against the act in the colonies.

In 1775, Henry delivered his "Liberty or Death" speech at the Virginia Convention, which galvanized Virginia's commitment to fight against Britain.

During the debates over ratification of the U.S. Constitution of 1787, Henry became one of America's leading Anti-Federalists, fearing that the Constitution represented a dangerous seizure of power by the national government.

From the Pen of Patrick Henry

"Let us not, I beseech you, sir, deceive ourselves. Sir, we have done everything that could be done to avert the storm which is now coming on. We have petitioned; we have remonstrated; we have supplicated; we have prostrated ourselves before the throne, and have implored its interposition to arrest the tyrannical hands of the ministry and

Parliament. Our petitions have been slighted; our remonstrances have produced additional violence and insult; our supplications have been disregarded; and we have been spurned, with contempt, from the foot of the throne! In vain, after these things, may we indulge the fond hope of peace and reconciliation. There is no longer any room for hope. If we wish to be free–if we mean to preserve inviolate those inestimable privileges for which we have been so long contending–if we mean not basely to abandon the noble struggle in which we have been so long engaged, and which we have pledged ourselves never to abandon until the glorious object of our contest shall be obtained–we must fight! I repeat it, sir, we must fight! An appeal to arms and to the God of hosts is all that is left us!

They tell us, sir, that we are weak; unable to cope with so formidable an adversary. But when shall we be stronger? Will it be the next week, or the next year? Will it be when we are totally disarmed, and when a British guard shall be stationed in every house? Shall we gather strength by irresolution and inaction? Shall we acquire the means of effectual resistance by lying supinely on our backs and hugging the delusive phantom of hope, until our enemies shall have bound us hand and foot? Sir, we are not weak if we make a proper use of those means which the God of nature hath placed in our power. The millions of people, armed in the holy cause of liberty, and in such a country as that which we possess, are invincible by any force which our enemy can send against us. Besides, sir, we shall not fight our battles alone. There is a just God who presides over the destinies of nations, and who will raise up friends to fight our battles for us. The battle, sir, is not to the strong alone; it is to the vigilant, the active, the brave. Besides, sir, we have no election. If we were base enough to desire it, it is now too late to retire from the contest. There is no retreat but in submission and slavery! Our chains are forged! Their clanking may be heard on the plains of Boston! The war is inevitable–and let it come! I repeat it, sir, let it come.

It is in vain, sir, to extenuate the matter. Gentlemen may cry, Peace, Peace– but there is no peace. The war is actually begun! The next gale that sweeps from the north will bring to our ears the clash of resounding arms! Our brethren are already in the field! Why stand we here idle? What is it that gentlemen wish? What would they have? Is life so dear, or peace so sweet, as to be purchased at the price of chains and slavery? Forbid it, Almighty God! I know not what course others may take; but as for me, give me liberty or give me death!"

–Patrick Henry, "Liberty or Death" speech (1775)

RECOMMENDED READING

Richard R. Beeman, *Patrick Henry: A Biography* (New York: McGraw-Hill, 1974).

William Wirt Henry, *Patrick Henry: Life, Correspondence, and Speeches* 3 vols. (New York: Charles Scribner's Sons, 1891).

Henry Mayer, *A Son of Thunder: Patrick Henry and the American Republic* (New York: F. Watts, 1986).

"There is not a single instance in history, in which civil liberty was lost, and religious liberty preserved entire. If therefore we yield up our temporal property, we at the same time deliver the conscience into bondage."

–John Witherspoon, "The Dominion of Providence over the Passions of Men," 1776.

"[T]he practice of true and undefiled religion . . . is the great foundation of public prosperity and national happiness."

–John Witherspoon, Congressional Thanksgiving Day Proclamation, 1782.

"[C]ivil liberty cannot be long preserved without virtue."

–John Witherspoon, "Sermon at a Public Thanksgiving," 1782.

JOHN WITHERSPOON
(1723-1794)

JEFFRY H. MORRISON

In 1774, John Adams, who had no patience for fools or preachers, called the Reverend John Witherspoon of Princeton a "clear, sensible" clergyman, and "as high a Son of Liberty, as any Man in America." Witherspoon's revolutionary activities between 1776 and 1783 would validate Adams's assessment. He served on New Jersey's committee of correspondence, and was the first man in that colony to call for independence from Great Britain. Witherspoon was appointed to the Second Continental Congress in late June 1776. He arrived in time to urge independence for the united colonies, and he was the only active clergyman to sign the Declaration of Independence. Indeed, he was the most influential political parson during America's Founding period. He was possibly the most active member of the Second Continental Congress during the Revolution, and was president of the College of New Jersey at Princeton during one of the most important quarter-centuries (1768-1794) in the whole of American history. In Explaining America, *Garry Wills noted that he was "probably the most influential teacher in the entire history of American education." In each of these roles–preacher, Patriot, college president–Witherspoon was outstanding. Writing more than a decade after Witherspoon's death, his old friend Benjamin Rush mused, "He was a man of a great and luminous mind. . . . His works will probably preserve his name to the end of time." His reputation continued high through the nineteenth century, but by the early twentieth century, the public began to forget the works and name of the parson-politician from New Jersey.*

John Witherspoon, D.D., LL.D., lived a remarkable life that spanned the last three quarters of the eighteenth century. Born the same year as Adam Smith at the dawn of the Scottish Enlightenment, he was educated at its heart at the University of Edinburgh. At the urging of Benjamin Rush, the trustees of the College of New Jersey at Princeton, and George Whitefield, the Anglican evangelist who helped touch off the First Great Awakening, Witherspoon emigrated to Princeton in 1768 to become the sixth president of the College. He remained there during the crucial founding years of the republic until his death in 1794. Witherspoon's political career was spent at the founding's epicenter–in and around Philadelphia during its crisis years. He served periodically in the New Jersey provincial and state legislatures (1774-89), in the Continental and Confederation Congresses throughout the Revolution (1776-82), and in the New Jersey convention that ratified the federal Constitution (1787). In signing the Declaration of Independence and the Articles of Confederation, and in ratifying the Constitution, Witherspoon had a direct hand in passing three of the four Organic Laws of the United States.

"Remarkable teacher of James Madison and a generation of mid-Atlantic elites who went to the college of New Jersey (Princeton) and made revolutionary republican ideals respectable."
–David Siemers

John Witherspoon had three careers, any one of which should have guaranteed him a prominent and lasting place in American history. As pastor, college president, and politician, his various careers combined in interesting ways. He was the only active clergyman and college president to sign the Declaration of Independence, which secured him a place that is literally unique among the Founders at the crossroads of religion, education and politics. Witherspoon was also an amateur scientist, political economist, rhetorician, and philosopher; in short, he was a polymath. His interests and abilities made him the sort of well-rounded man we associate with American Enlightenment characters like Thomas Jefferson or Benjamin Franklin. Like those two, Witherspoon was an intellectual handyman with a scientific bent; for instance, he was elected an officer in Franklin's American Philosophical Society the same year as Jefferson and the astronomer David Rittenhouse. But unlike those colleagues in the Society, Witherspoon added the roles of theologian and moral philosopher to his scientific and political interests.

By the summer of 1776, when he led the New Jersey delegation to the Second Continental Congress in Philadelphia, Witherspoon had already been active in provincial politics for several years. He had been on the committee of correspondence from Somerset County since its inception, and had been a delegate to the New Jersey provincial congress from 1774 until his appointment to the Continental Congress in June 1776. His record in the Congress reveals that, excepting part of the year 1780, Witherspoon was scrupulous in his attendance and almost preternaturally active. The *Journals of the Continental Congress* record Witherspoon's appointment to 126 committees in his six years of service, including two crucial "standing" or permanent committees, the Committee on Foreign Affairs and the Board of War. Witherspoon got the attention of his congressional colleagues early and held it throughout the next six years. Sometime during the debates on July 1 and 2, 1776, a member of the conservative faction (probably John Dickinson of Pennsylvania) argued that the country at large was not yet ripe for independence. Witherspoon promptly responded that in his judgment, the colonies were not only ripe for independence but "in danger of becoming rotten for the want of it." By so replying, he helped prod Congress toward passing Richard Henry Lee's Resolution for Independence on July 2, and the Declaration of Independence two days later. Appointment to a prodigious number of committees followed immediately, and did not abate until Witherspoon retired from Congress at the end of 1782. It is a further measure of the confidence other congressmen placed in him that Witherspoon was tapped to draw up the instructions to the American peace commission in France in 1781.

Witherspoon also made less formal, though no less important, contributions to the Founding. He preached a number of politically influential sermons, and was a productive pamphleteer, especially during the Revolutionary period. Several of his political pamphlets and speeches have been preserved in his *Works*, including: "Reflections on the Present State of Public Affairs"; "On Conducting the American Controversy"; "On the Contest Between Great Britain and America"; "On the Affairs of the United States"; a piece on Thomas Paine's *Common Sense* over the pseudonym "Aristides"; and a series of periodical essays which he signed "the Druid."

Nor did Witherspoon's political influence end with his own retirement from politics in 1789. The list of his Princeton graduates reads like a roll of early American notables. Among these were twelve members of the Continental Congress, five delegates to the

Constitutional Convention, one U.S. president (James Madison), a vice president (Aaron Burr), seventy-seven U.S. Congressmen, three Supreme Court Justices, eight U.S. District Court Judges, one Secretary of State, three Attorneys General, and two foreign ministers. In addition to these national office holders, twenty-six of Witherspoon's graduates were state judges, seventeen were members of their state constitutional conventions, and fourteen were delegates to the state conventions that ratified the Constitution. Chief among Witherspoon's graduates was, of course, James Madison, Father of the Constitution and reluctant architect of the Bill of Rights. Madison stayed on an extra term following his graduation to study Hebrew and the law under the "old Doctor's" direction, and then proceeded to carry certain elements of Witherspoon's political-theological creed into his own public career, culminating in two stormy terms as President from 1809-17.

So intertwined were Witherspoon's political and pastoral careers, not to mention his political theory and his theology, that his political career cannot adequately be appreciated without understanding his status as a clergyman. Witherspoon came from a long and distinguished line of Reformed (i.e. Calvinist) pastors, and his mother claimed lineal descent from the Scottish reformer John Knox. In Britain and Europe, he had gained fame as the outspoken leader of the democratic and evangelical Popular party that opposed the more traditional (though theologically liberal) Moderate party of Frances Hutcheson in the Scottish Presbyterian church, and as the author of two widely-cited satirical pieces written during his Scottish ministry. Thus, by the time he received the call to Princeton in 1768, Witherspoon was already something of an international figure in ecclesiastical circles.

His reputation continued to rise in America. He quickly formed powerful connections throughout the colonies, from fellow pastors like Ezra Stiles and Timothy Dwight in New England, to family–one of his daughters married Madison's friend the Reverend Samuel Stanhope Smith, who founded what became Hampden-Sydney College in Virginia and years later succeeded Witherspoon as president of Princeton–and Presbyterian colleagues in the Carolinas and Georgia. Doctor Witherspoon was a fixture in the joint conventions the Presbyterians had with the Congregationalists of the General Association of Connecticut. These conventions were originally convened to ally the two denominations against a potential Anglican establishment, that perennial bugaboo of dissenting colonial Protestants. There his lifelong friendship with the Reverend Ezra Stiles, the president of Yale College who found Witherspoon "a very learned divine" but complained privately that he was too much of a politician, was strengthened.

From 1785 through 1789, Reverend Witherspoon was the leading figure in nationalizing the American Presbyterian Church. Out of that nationalization came catechisms, a confession, a directory of worship, and an ecclesiastical constitution called "the Form of the Government," of which portions were written by Witherspoon. His introduction to the Form of the Government set out the first principles of church polity for the new national church. Due primarily to his influence, the Form of the Government contained articles which strongly upheld religious liberty, and in fact liberalized the Westminster Confession of Faith of 1647.

His denominational and national prominence gave Witherspoon's sermons, many of which were printed and circulated extensively, considerable weight. Weightiest of all was his first explicitly political sermon, "The Dominion of Providence Over the Passions of Men," preached on the 17th of May, 1776, a congressional fast day. The first edition of "The Dominion of Providence" was printed that year by Robert Aitken of Philadelphia, whose congressionally-approved edition of the Bible would later become the first English Bible printed in North America. Second and third editions of the sermon were reprinted in Glasgow in 1777, accompanied by annotations in which Witherspoon was called a rebel and a traitor; a fourth was reprinted in Philadelphia and London in 1777, and a fifth was brought out in London in 1779. The overwhelmingly favorable American response to the sermon helped rally support for independence, especially in New Jersey, which was not keen on independence just then, and vaulted Witherspoon into the Continental Congress in late June of 1776. As the *de facto* head of the New Jersey delegation in Congress, and of all colonial Presbyterians, Witherspoon was ideally positioned to spur the independence movement forward.

> "He was a real workhorse in the revolutionary cause as well as a teacher to many of the new nation's principal leaders, including James Madison. As a Founding Father, he plays second fiddle to none!"
> – Thomas Buckley

In addition to the "Dominion of Providence" and his other political sermons, Witherspoon was the author of one congressional fast day proclamation and two thanksgiving day proclamations, fully a third of Congress's religious proclamations during the years he was a member of that body. These proclamations are quintessential examples of the theological-political ethos of the revolutionary years. Many of their themes–the Almighty's providential care for the United States, the necessity of religion and morality for civic health–were the stock-in-trade of late eighteenth century American political orations like Washington's Farewell Address. Witherspoon incorporated those proclamation themes in his sermons and lectures to upperclassmen and divinity students.

In addition to his duties as President of the College of New Jersey, Witherspoon taught the capstone course on moral philosophy to graduating seniors, as well as courses on rhetoric, history, and divinity. It is commonly acknowledged that the Lectures on Eloquence, first given as class lectures by President Witherspoon and later published in his *Works* beginning in 1800-01, were "the first American rhetorical treatise." In fact, Witherspoon was responsible for a number of "firsts" in America. He published a series of essays from 1776 to 1781 under the pseudonym "the Druid," in which he included observations on the American language and even coined the word "Americanism." Witherspoon has also been attributed with introducing the Latin word "campus" into the American lexicon, when he used it to describe the grounds at Princeton in 1774. But President Witherspoon's Lectures on Moral Philosophy marked a critical first in American higher education: a systematic treatment of moral philosophy, which was then coming into vogue in the colonial colleges. Derived largely, though not lavishly, from Francis Hutcheson's *System of Moral Philosophy* (1755), these lectures of Witherspoon's–in oral, manuscript, and published forms–were vastly influential. Manuscripts of the lectures, which were copied verbatim from a syllabus by each member of the senior class at Princeton for a quarter century, circulated widely throughout the colonies. In 1820, the University of Pennsylvania was still listing "Witherspoon," along with "Hutcheson, Paley [and] Smith" as a text on "natural and political law."

Throughout the Revolution, Witherspoon had continuously traveled between Princeton and Philadelphia, teaching and presiding over the College, preaching and ministering in the local Presbyterian church and in the synod of New York and Philadelphia, attending sessions of Congress, and even visiting the Continental Army in the field. His energy was unflagging in the midst of personal hardship, including the death of one of his sons, who was killed at the battle of Germantown. But the end of the Revolution left the College in a shambles. Nassau Hall had been plundered by the British and Hessians, enrollment was down drastically, and so were the College's financial affairs.

During the Confederation period, Witherspoon set about rebuilding the College and re-entered New Jersey politics. In 1787, he was a leader of the New Jersey ratifying convention, and spearheaded the early ratification of the Constitution, which was unanimous. Following ratification, Witherspoon's health began to decline, though apparently not his vigor; after the death of his wife, he raised Princeton eyebrows by marrying a twenty-four year old widow who bore him two more children in his old age. As his eyesight failed along with his general health, Witherspoon turned over control of the College to his son-in-law Samuel Stanhope Smith, though the Old Doctor retained the title of President and some of its incumbent duties. John Witherspoon died at Princeton in 1794, having lived a life that suggests he be removed from the roll of Forgotten Founders.

MAIN CONTRIBUTIONS OF JOHN WITHERSPOON

Witherspoon was the only active clergyman and college president to sign the Declaration of Independence.

Witherspoon had a direct hand in passing three of the four Organic Laws of the United States: the Declaration of Independence, the Articles of Confederation, and the Constitution.

As president and professor of moral philosophy at Princeton during the critical years of the Founding (1768-94), Witherspoon helped produce the most important and impressive leadership generation in American history, including a U.S. president (James Madison, who stayed an extra term after graduation to be tutored by Witherspoon), a vice president, seventy-seven congressmen, and three Supreme Court justices, along with many state and local office holders.

From the Pen of John Witherspoon

"Whereas, it hath pleased Almighty God, the father of mercies, remarkably to assist and support the United States of America in their important struggle for liberty, against the long continued efforts of a powerful nation: it is the duty of all ranks to observe and thankfully acknowledge the interpositions of his Providence in their behalf. Through the whole of the contest, from its first rise to this time, the influence of Divine Providence may be clearly perceived in many signal instances, of which we mention but a few.

In revealing the councils of our enemies, when the discoveries were seasonable and important, and the means seemingly inadequate or fortuitous; in preserving and even improving the union of the several States, on the breach of which our enemies placed their greatest dependence; in increasing the number and adding to the zeal and attachment of the friends of Liberty; in granting remarkable deliverances, and blessing us with the most signal success, when affairs seemed to have the most discouraging appearance; in raising up for us a powerful and generous ally, in one of the first of the European powers; in confounding the councils of our enemies, and suffering them to pursue such measures as have most directly contributed to frustrate their own desires and expectations; above all, in making their extreme cruelty to the inhabitants of these States, when in their power, and their savage devastation of property, the very means of cementing our union, and adding vigor to every effort in opposition to them.

And as we cannot help leading the good people of these States to a retrospect on the events which have taken place since the beginning of the war, so we recommend in a particular manner to their observation, the goodness of God in the year now drawing to a conclusion; in which the Confederation of the United States has been completed, in which there have been so many instances of prowess and success in our armies; particularly in the Southern States, where, notwithstanding the difficulties with which they had to struggle, they have recovered the whole country which the enemy had overrun, leaving them only a post or two on or near the sea; in which we have been so powerfully and effectually assisted by our allies, while in all the conjunct operations the most perfect harmony has subsisted in the allied army; in which there has been so plentiful a harvest, and so great abundance of the fruits of the earth of every kind, as not only enables us easily to supply the wants of the army, but gives comfort and happiness to the whole people; and in which, after the success of our allies by sea, a General of the first Rank, with his whole army, has been captured by the allied forces under the direction of our Commander in Chief.

It is therefore recommended to the several states to set apart the thirteenth day of December next, to be religiously observed as a Day of Thanksgiving and Prayer; that all the people may assemble on that day, with grateful hearts, to celebrate the praise of our gracious Benefactor; to confess our manifold sins; to offer up our most fervent supplications to the God of all grace, that it may please Him to pardon our offences, and incline our hearts for the future to keep all his laws; to comfort and relieve all our brethren who are in distress or captivity; to prosper all husbandmen, and give success to all engaged in lawful commerce; to impart wisdom and integrity to our counsellors, judgment and fortitude to our officers and soldiers; to protect and prosper our illustrious ally, and favor our united exertions for the speedy establishment of a safe, honorable and lasting peace; and bless all seminaries of learning; and cause the knowledge of God to cover the earth, as the water covers the seas."

–John Witherspoon, Congressional Thanksgiving Day Proclamation (October 26, 1781)

RECOMMENDED READING

Varnum Lansing Collins, *President Witherspoon: A Biography.* 2 vols. (Princeton: Princeton University Press, 1925; repr. New York: Arno Press, 1969).

Jeffry H. Morrison, *John Witherspoon and the Founding of the American Republic* (Notre Dame, IN: University of Notre Dame Press, 2005).

L. Gordon Tait, *The Piety of John Witherspoon: Pew, Pulpit, and Public Forum.* (Louisville, KY: Geneva Press, 2001).

John Witherspoon, *The Selected Writings of John Witherspoon.* Ed. Thomas Miller. (Carbondale: Southern Illinois University Press, 1990).

CONCLUSION
America's *Other* Forgotten Founders

MARK DAVID HALL AND GARY L. GREGG II

It is difficult to imagine a course today covering the American Founding that does not consider the contributions of women and racial minorities. Because they were either formally or informally banned from holding political offices, it was harder for them to directly affect public policy. However, a burgeoning literature has demonstrated that educated women often exercised significant personal influence or were able to make a substantial impact through their writings. Participants in the first round of the survey suggested a number of women whom they believed should be remembered today, including Abigail Adams, Mercy Otis Warren, Dolley Payne Madison, Judith Sargent Murray, and Phillis Wheatley.

We were somewhat surprised that neither Abigail Adams nor Mercy Otis Warren were included among the top ten forgotten Founders (the top thirty list included Dolley Madison and Mercy Warren, but not Abigail Adams). We suspect that many respondents did not consider Abigail to be "forgotten." Scholars and popular authors alike have noted that she had a fine, penetrating mind and that she offered political advice to her husband. She is certainly well known for her March 1776 letter to John Adams, then serving in Congress, in which she encouraged him to:

> "Remember the Ladies, and be more generous and

favourable to them than your ancestors. Do not put such unlimited power into the hands of the Husbands. Remember all Men would be tyrants if they could. If perticular care and attention is not paid to the Ladies we are determined to foment a Rebelion, and will not hold ourselves bound by any Laws in which we have no voice, or Representation."

Mercy Otis Warren is less well known than Abigail, but she was more directly involved in political debates through her public writings (although she often wrote under a pseudonym). Survey participant Carol Berkin observed that she was a "key propagandist for radicals in Massachusetts, [and] wrote the first history of the Revolution." As well, she regularly corresponded with a range of political leaders, and in 1788, she published an essay entitled "Observations on the New Constitution," which argued against ratification of the proposed Constitution.

Adams and Warren were learned women who had immediate or indirect access to a range of American political leaders. One respondent, who declined to be identified or participate further in our study, suggested that "the forgotten Founders are: every Patriot woman who stayed home and took care of farms & families while their husbands and sons were away fighting in the Revolutionary War or serving overseas as a diplomat or in the Continental Congress."

We agree that these women, like their better known elite sisters, should not be forgotten.

Even more than white women, racial minorities in the Founding

Era were excluded from positions of public influence. But that did not mean that they did not contribute to America's Founding. One intriguing suggestion for approaching these Founders is to focus on a representative of a group. For instance, law professor William R. Casto suggested that Jack Arabas be included as an important forgotten Founder, explaining:

> I view Jack Arabas as a representative of the black soldiers who fought for America's freedom in the Revolutionary War. Arabas was a slave whose owner put him in the Connecticut Continental Line in 1777 in exchange for a bounty. When the war was over six years later, his owner reclaimed him. Jack ran off and was arrested as a runaway slave in New Haven. The Connecticut Superior Court, however, declared that Arabas' service made him a free man. He lived the rest of his life in New Haven.

Conversely, political science professor Alan Gibson proposed "Colonel Tye, the slave Titus, who fought with the British against the Revolutionaries. Most slaves who fought in the Revolution fought for the British. This is a very unrecognized aspect of the American Revolution." Ideally, it seems to us, both Arabas and Tye, or similar "representatives" of these groups, should be discussed in any course covering the Revolution.

Casto and Gibson gently challenged the individualistic bias of our survey, but Bruce Johansen more directly pointed out that:

Your form seems tailored to individual names, not a confederacy of nations such as the Iroquois. That being the case, I would select two Iroquois leaders. One was Canassatego, the Tahadaho (speaker) of the Confederacy, who admonished the colonist to unite on a federal model as early as 1744 . . . another Iroquois leader, whom the English call Hendrick (his Native name was Tiyanoga) was invited to the Albany Congress to advise the colonial delegates on how the Iroquois Confederacy operates.

We agree that the possible influence of the Iroquois on the American Founding is worthy of consideration, and we appreciate as well the comment made by Colin G. Calloway of Dartmouth College that students of the Founding should consider Native Americans such as Dragging Canoe, Cornstalk, White Eyes, and Nancy Ward, who are an important (and often sad) part of the story of the westward expansion of Americans of European descent.

Numerous survey participants suggested that ministers have been unjustly neglected in the study of the American Founding. John Witherspoon, it is true, made our list of top ten forgotten Founders, but we wonder if he would be on it if he had not been the only active clergyman to sign the Declaration of Independence. This event was certainly significant, but more important still were the thousands of sermons preached by Witherspoon, his contemporaries, and his predecessors that directly or indirectly encouraged Americans to protect their God-given rights, support government by consent of the governed, and guard against the concentration of power in the hands of sinful creatures. One of our respondents, Marvin Olasky, Provost of The King's College and Editor-in-Chief of *World*, contended that:

> George Whitefield became a grandfather of the American Revolution when he argued that Christian subjects must obey divine laws and could, if necessary, break laws that pressed them to do wrong . . . One of Whitefield's followers, Elisha Williams, played out such thought at greater length in a pamphlet published in 1744 "The Essential Rights and Liberties of Protestants."

Other ministers suggested by respondents include Ezra Stiles, Samuel Miller, William White, David Griffith, Bishop James Madison, George Duffield, John Leland, Isaac Backus, and John and Frederick Muhlenberg.

Finally, a significant group about which many respondents were passionate was the Anti-Federalists. The Anti-Federalists consisted of a diverse group of political figures who, in general, opposed the concentration of power in a strong central government, supported vital state and local governments, advocated a clear articulation of rights, and opposed ratification of the proposed national constitution of 1787. In addition to the two Anti-Federalists who made our top ten list of forgotten Founders (George Mason and Patrick Henry), survey participants suggested, among others: (1) Richard Henry Lee, who, according to Howard Lubert, clearly belongs in the "pantheon of Founders," if he is the author of the "Federal Farmer." In a similar vein, Walter Nicgorski contended that Lee, "or whomever wrote the 'Federal Farmer,'"[offered] "intelligent and far-seeing objections to the proposed Constitution, a match for Publius in his coherence and depth." (2) Robert Yates, who, according to Terence Ball, likely "became the pseudonymous 'Brutus,' who published an influential series of sixteen letters opposing ratification. Many of the pro-Constitution arguments and defenses offered by 'Publius' in *The Federalist* are direct replies and responses to Brutus." Likewise, Gordon Lloyd wrote that Brutus's essays "are the best ever written that warned about the potential dangers of inadequate representation, the absence of a Bill of Rights, and the power of the Judiciary in the original Constitution. (3) Melancton Smith, who, according to Ralph Ketcham, was the "most important Anti-Federalist theorist and spokesman." (4) Luther Martin, who, E. Christian Kopff argued, "was the most articulate and learned of the defenders of the rights and sovereignty of states." (5) John Taylor of Carolina, who, Garrett Ward Sheldon noted, was a "[l]eading Anti-Federalist . . . [who] wrote extensively on constitutionalism, economics, agriculture, slavery, and rights."

We quote extensively (but not comprehensively) from supporters of different Anti-Federalists to help communicate how strongly many survey respondents thought their contributions to the creation of the American republic have been neglected. As noted above, men and women on the "losing" side of history are often neglected by history texts, but at least among our respondents, there seems to be a consensus that the Anti-Federalists should be seriously considered in courses covering the Founding Era.

Conclusion

The primary purpose of our survey and this book is to promote a broader discussion of America's Founding Period. The survey reveals that there is a significant scholarly consensus that a number of important Founders have been unjustly neglected. Exploring the thoughts and actions of these men is a good place to begin a larger conversation. A robust and accurate treatment of America's Founders, however, must move beyond the fifteen or so men intimately involved in promoting the Revolution and Constitution to include the wide range of men and women who helped make America what it is today.

APPENDIX A
Contributors

Henry J. Abraham is James Hart Professor Emeritus of Government and Foreign Affairs at the University of Virginia whose numerous books include *Justices, Presidents, and Senators: A History of the U.S. Supreme Court Appointments from Washington to Clinton; Freedom and the Court: Civil Rights and Liberties in the United States;* and *The Judicial Process: An Introductory Analysis of the Courts of the United States, England, and France.* As a pioneer in comparative judicial studies, Dr. Abraham has served as a Fulbright Scholar in Denmark and has lectured throughout the world.

John Bush, a graduate of Vanderbilt University and Harvard Law School, practices law in the Louisville office of Greenebaum, Doll & McDonald PLLC. Mr. Bush is currently writing a book about Gouverneur Morris.

Daniel L. Dreisbach is Professor in the School of Public Affairs at American University in Washington, D.C. Professor Dreisbach's principal research interests include American constitutional law and history, First Amendment law, church-state relations, and criminal procedure. He has written extensively on these topics and has authored or edited seven books, including *Thomas Jefferson and the Wall of Separation between Church and State* (New York Univ. Press, 2002). He has published over fifty book chapters, reviews, and articles in scholarly journals, including *American Journal of Legal History, Emory Law Journal, Journal of Church and State, North Carolina Law Review,* and *William and Mary Quarterly.*

Gary L. Gregg, II holds the Mitch McConnell Chair in Leadership at the University of Louisville where he is also director of the McConnell Center for Political Leadership. He is the author or editor of seven books including *The Presidential Republic: Executive Representation and Deliberative Democracy; Securing Democracy: Why We Have an Electoral College;* and *Thinking about the Presidency.* He is also author of a new fiction series for young adult readers called *The Remnant Chronicles,* the first installment of which was published as *The Sporran.*

Mark David Hall is Herbert Hoover Distinguished Professor of Political Science at George Fox University. He has written *The Political and Legal Philosophy of James Wilson, 1742-1798* and co-edited the *Collected Works of James Wilson* (2 vol.) and *The Founders on God and Government.* He is currently writing a book entitled, *The Old Puritan and a New Nation: Roger Sherman and the Creation of the American Republic,* and is co-editing *The Forgotten Founders on Religion and Public Life* and *The Sacred Rights of Conscience: Selected Readings on Religious Liberty and Church-State Relations in the American Founding.*

Jonathan Den Hartog is an Assistant Professor of History at Northwestern College (St. Paul, MN). A specialist in American political and religious history, he received his doctorate from the

University of Notre Dame in 2006. He is currently working on a book manuscript examining the religious dimension of Federalist party politics.

Thomas S. Kidd is associate professor of history at Baylor University, and a resident scholar at Baylor's Institute for Studies of Religion. He is the author of *American Christians and Islam: Evangelical Culture and Muslims from the Colonial Period to the Age of Global Terrorism* (Princeton, 2008); *The Great Awakening: The Roots of Evangelical Christianity in Colonial America* (Yale, 2007); and *The Protestant Interest: New England after Puritanism* (Yale, 2004).

Howard L. Lubert is Associate Professor of Political Science at James Madison University where he teaches courses in American political thought and political theory. Dr. Lubert was the recipient of a 2004 National Endowment for the Humanities award for his ongoing study of federalism in the American Founding. He is co-editor of the two-volume anthology, *Classics of American Political and Constitutional Thought* (Hackett, 2007), and has published essays on the political thought of James Otis and Thomas Hutchinson (American colonial leaders), John Dickinson, and Benjamin Franklin. His most recent publication is "The New York Constitution: Emerging Principles in American Constitutional Thought," published in *American Constitutionalism in the Fifty States* (University of Missouri Press, 2008).

Jeffry H. Morrison is Associate Professor of Government at

Regent University and a faculty member at the federal government's James Madison Foundation in Washington, D.C. He has also held faculty appointments at Princeton University, the U.S. Air Force Academy, and Georgetown University. He graduated with distinction from Boston College and from Georgetown, where he received his Ph.D. His work has been published or is forthcoming with Johns Hopkins University Press, Columbia University Press, the University of Notre Dame Press, Rowman & Littlefield, and Cambridge University Press. His books include *The Founders on God and Government* (2004), *John Witherspoon and the Founding of the American Republic* (2005), and *The Political Philosophy of George Washington* (forthcoming in 2009).

Barbara A. Perry is the Carter Glass Professor of Government and Founding executive director of the Center for Civic Renewal and the Virginia Law-Related Education Center at Sweet Briar College. Dr. Perry served as the Senior Fellow for Civics Education at the McConnell Center for 2006-2007. In addition to publishing nearly thirty articles, she has authored eight books, including *Jacqueline Kennedy: First Lady of the New Frontier* (University Press of Kansas, 2004) and *The Priestly Tribe: The Supreme Court's Image in the American Mind* (Praeger, 1999). Her most recent book is *The Michigan Affirmative Action Cases* (University Press of Kansas, 2007).

David Voelker is Assistant Professor of Humanistic Studies and History at the University of Wisconsin–Green Bay, where he has been teaching since 2003. He has written on Orestes Brownson, Thomas Paine's religion, and on religion and reform in the early United States. He is also active in the scholarship of teaching and learning history.

APPENDIX B
The Forgotten Founders

THE COMPLETE LIST OF NOMINATED PEOPLE
FROM THE AMERICAN FOUNDING

Roger Sherman
James Wilson
George Mason
John Dickinson
Gouverneur Morris
John Witherspoon
John Jay
Mclancton Smith
Richard Henry Lee
Oliver Ellsworth
Benjamin Rush
James Iredell
James Otis
Thomas Paine
Elbridge Gerry
Luther Martin
Robert Yates
Bishop James Madison
Brutus
Dolley Payne Madison
Elias Boudinot
Elisha Williams
Ezra Stiles
Fredrick Augustus Mohlenbery
John Marshall
Mercy Otis Warren

Edmund Randolph
Fischer Ames
Francis Marion
George Duffield
George Whitefield
George Wythe
Isaac Backus
Jack Arabas
James Monroe
John Allen
John Carroll
John Lansing
John Leland
John McDonald
John Ross
John Rutledge of SC
John Stuart
John Taylor
Joseph Brant
Nancy Ward
Nathaniel Macon
Pelatiah Webster
Penelope Burke
Philip Freneau
Phillis Wheatley
Robert Morris

Nathaniel Greene
Patrick Henry
Samuel Adams
Aaron Burr
Albert Gallatin
Anthony Benezet
Charles Penchney
Colonel Tye
Cornstalk
David Griffith
Dragging Canoe

Samuel Langdon
Samuel Miller
Samuel Sherwood
Tench Coxe
Theophilus Parsons
White Eyes
William Findley
William Paterson
William Richardson Davie
William White

APPENDIX C
The Forgotten Founders

Rank	Name	Total Points
1	James Wilson	214
2	George Mason	152
3	Gouverneur Morris	128
4	John Jay	125
5	Roger Sherman	124
6	John Marshall	117
7	John Dickinson	92
8	Thomas Paine	76
9	Patrick Henry	71
10	John Witherspoon	68
11	Samuel Adams	66
12	Melancton Smith	55
13	Benjamin Rush	52
14	James Iredell	37
15	Oliver Ellsworth	36
16	Richard Henry Lee	34
17	James Otis	33
18	Elbridge Gerry	32

Rank	Name	Total Points
19	Luther Martin	31
20	Nathaniel Greene	30
21	Fisher Ames (tie)	19
21	Robert Yates (tie)	19
23	Bishop James Madison	13
24	Elisha Williams (tie)	12
24	Dolley Paine Todd Madison (tie)	12
24	John Leland (tie)	12
27	Fredrick Augustus Muhlenberg	6
28	Mercy Otis Warren	5
29	Elias Boudinot	4
30	Ezra Stiles	1

APPENDIX D

The 45 Scholars Who Participated in the Forgotten Founders Project

Henry J. Abraham is James Hart Professor Emeritus of Government and Foreign Affairs at the University of Virginia whose numerous books include *Justices, Presidents, and Senators: A History of the U.S. Supreme Court Appointments from Washington to Clinton; Freedom and the Court: Civil Rights and Liberties in the United States;* and *The Judicial Process: An Introductory Analysis of the Courts of the United States, England, and France.* As a pioneer in comparative judicial studies, Dr. Abraham has served as a Fulbright Scholar in Denmark and has lectured throughout the world.

William B. Allen is Professor of Political Philosophy at Michigan State University. Dr. Allen served as Director of the State Council of Higher Education for Virginia from June 1998 through August 1999, while on leave from Michigan State. Previously, Dr. Allen served as Dean and Professor at James College at Michigan State University. Dr. Allen has authored or edited several books including *George Washington: A Collection. Re-Thinking Uncle Tom: The Political Philosophy of H. B. Stowe* will appear in 2008, as also *George Washington: America's First Progressive* and *The Personal and the Political: Three Fables of Montesquieu.* He previously published *Habits of Mind: Fostering Access and Excellence in Higher Education* (with Carol M. Allen).

Terence Ball received his Ph.D. from the University of California at Berkeley and was for many years Professor of Political Science at the

University of Minnesota. He is currently Professor of Political Science at Arizona State University. Dr. Ball has held visiting professorships at the University of California at San Diego, Cambridge University, and Oxford University. In addition to many articles in scholarly journals, he is the author of six books, including *Transforming Political Discourse* (1998), *Reappraising Political Theory* (1995), and a mystery novel, *Rousseau's Ghost* (1998). He has also edited or co-edited eleven books, including, *The Federalist* (2003) and the *Cambridge History of Twentieth-Century Political Thought* (2003).

Ryan J. Barrilleaux is Professor and Chair of the Political Science Department at Miami University (Ohio) and the Editor-in-Chief of *Catholic Social Science Review*. He is the author or editor of numerous books and scholarly articles including *The Post-Modern Presidency: The Office After Ronald Reagan* (1988) and *Presidential Frontiers: Underexplored Issues in White House Politics* (1998).

Carol Berkin is Presidential Professor of History at Baruch College and The Graduate Center, CUNY. She teaches early American and women's history. Her publications include: *Jonathan Sewall: Odyssey of an American Loyalist* (1974); *First Generations: Women of Colonial America* (1996); *A Brilliant Solution: Inventing the American Constitution* (2002); and *Revolutionary Mothers: Women in the Struggle for American Independence* (2005). Dr. Berkin has also appeared as a commentator on screen in the PBS series by Ric Burns, "New York" and in the MPH series, "The Founding Fathers," in 2000, and in Middlemarch Productions', "Liberty! The American Revolution" and "Benjamin Franklin."

R. B. Bernstein is Distinguished Adjunct Professor of Law at New York Law School and the author or editor of nearly 20 books on American constitutional history, including *Are We to Be a Nation: The Making of the Constitution* (1987) and *Amending America* (1995), both nominated for the Pulitzer, Bancroft, and Parkman Prizes. His recent book, *Thomas Jefferson* (2003), called "the best short biography of Jefferson ever written" by Gordon S. Wood in The New York Times Book Review, also was nominated for the Pulitzer, Bancroft, and Parkman Prizes.

Thomas Buckley is Professor of American Religious History at the Jesuit School of Theology at Berkeley. Dr. Buckley's research interests are in the history of church-state relations with an emphasis on Thomas Jefferson's writings and the interaction of religion with government policy in the United States. He is the author of *Church and State in Revolutionary Virginia, 1776-1787* (Virginia, 1977) and *"The Great Catastrophe of My Life": Divorce in the Old Dominion* (North Carolina, 2002), and he is the editor of *"If You Love That Lady Don't Marry Her": The Courtship Letters of Sally McDowell and John Miller, 1854-1856* (Missouri, 2000). He is currently working on a study of the church-state relationship in Virginia from Jamestown to 1940.

Colin G. Calloway is Professor of History, Samson Occom Professor of Native American Studies, and Chair of the Native American Studies program at Dartmouth College. Dr. Calloway is the winner of the 2004 Caroline Bancroft History Prize for his book, *One Vast Winter Count: The Native American West Before Lewis and Clark.* Dr. Calloway received his Ph.D. from the University of Leeds in England in 1978. He first came to Dartmouth College as a visiting professor in 1990, and he became a permanent member of the faculty in 1995.

William R. Casto is the Paul Whitfield Horn University Professor, which is the highest honor that the Texas Tech University may bestow on members of its faculty. Texas Tech has also honored him with the Texas Tech President's Academic Achievement Award and the President's Excellence in Teaching Award. The United States Supreme Court frequently cites Dr. Casto's scholarship. He has written three well-received books: *The Supreme Court in the Early Republic, Oliver Ellsworth and the Creation of the Federal Republic,* and *Foreign Affairs and the Constitution in the Age of Fighting Sail.*

Lee Cheek is the Chair of the Social and Behavioral Sciences Division and Professor of Political Science and Philosophy at Brewton-Parker College in Mt. Vernon, Georgia. He is a scholar of American political theory generally, and more specifically of John C. Calhoun's political thought. From 2000 to 2005, Dr. Cheek served as Associate Professor of Political Science at Lee University. His books include *Calhoun and Popular Rule, Political Philosophy and Cultural Renewal,* and *Order and Legitimacy,* among others. He has also served as a congressional aide and as a political consultant.

Christopher Collier was Professor of American History at the University of Bridgeport in Connecticut until 1984. Dr. Collier was also a Professor of History at the University of Connecticut from 1984 to 2000. He is now Professor Emeritus in both capacities. Dr. Collier was nominated for a Pulitzer Prize for his book, *Roger Sherman's Connecticut: Yankee Politics and the American Revolution.* He also published *All Politics Is Local: Family, Friends, and Provincial Interests in the Creation of the Constitution* (2003), and with James Lincoln Collier, *Decision In Philadelphia* (1985). In addition, he published eight historical novels for young adults, a 23-volume history of the United States for middle school students, and many articles on the legal and constitutional history of the U.S. and Connecticut.

Daniel L. Dreisbach is Professor in the School of Public Affairs at American University in Washington, D.C. Professor Dreisbach's principal research interests include American constitutional law and history, First Amendment law, church-state relations, and criminal procedure. He has written extensively on these topics and has authored or edited seven books, including *Thomas Jefferson and the Wall of Separation between Church and State* (New York Univ. Press, 2002). He has published over fifty book chapters, reviews, and articles in scholarly journals, including *American Journal of Legal History, Emory Law Journal, Journal of Church and State, North Carolina Law Review*, and *William and Mary Quarterly*.

Michael Federici is Professor of Political Science at Mercyhurst College (PA) and Director of The Center for Constitutional Studies at the National Humanities Institute in Washington, DC. A frequent contributor to scholarly journals, he is the author of *The Challenge of Populism: The Rise of Right-Wing Democratism in Postwar America* (1991) and *Eric Voegelin: The Restoration of Order* (2002). He has a forthcoming book, an edited volume of Orestes Brownson's political writings (ISI Books), due out in late 2008 or early 2009. His teaching and research areas include American Government, Constitutional Law, Civil Liberties, and Political Theory.

Matthew J. Franck is Professor and Department Chair of Political Science at Radford University (VA) and a 2008-09 Visiting Fellow in the James Madison Program at Princeton University. A former Salvatori Fellow with the Heritage Foundation and Fulbright Professor of American Studies at Yonsei University in Seoul, South Korea, he is the author of *Against the Imperial Judiciary: The Supreme Court vs. the Sovereignty of the People* (Kansas, 1996) and the co-editor of *Sober as a Judge: The Supreme Court and Republican Liberty* (Rowman and Littlefield, 1999).

Bruce Frohnen is Associate Professor of Law at Ave Maria School of Law in Ann Arbor, Michigan and Senior Fellow at the Russell Kirk Center for Cultural Renewal. Dr. Frohnen was a resident scholar with the Heritage Foundation and a senior fellow with the Liberty Fund. He also spent five years as a legislative aid to former U.S. Senator Spencer Abraham. Prior to joining the Ave Maria faculty, Dr. Frohnen served as a visiting scholar at the Johns Hopkins School of Advanced International Studies.

Richard Gamble is Anna Margaret Ross Alexander Professor of History and Political Science and Associate Professor of History at Hillsdale College. In 2003, he spent two terms as a Visiting Scholar at St. Edmund's College, Cambridge University. His essays and reviews have appeared in *The Journal of Southern History, Orbis, Humanitas, The Intercollegiate Review*, and *The Independent Review*. He is the author of *The War for Righteousness: Progressive Christianity, the Great War, and the Rise of the Messianic Nation* (ISI Books, 2003) and compiler and editor of the forthcoming anthology, *The Great Tradition: Classic Readings on What It Means to be an Educated Human Being* (ISI Books, 2007).

Scott Douglas Gerber is Ella and Ernest Chair in Law and Professor of Law in the Claude W. Pettit College of Law at Ohio Northern University. Dr. Gerber is also Senior Research Scholar in Law and Politics at the Social Philosophy and Policy Center. He has published six books and nearly one hundred articles, book reviews, op-eds, and sundry pieces.

Alan Gibson is Professor of Political Science at California State University–Chico. His teaching and research interests focus on the political thought of James Madison and the study of the American Founding. He has published articles in *Polity, History of Political Thought, The Review of Politics,* and *The Political Science Reviewer.* Most recently, Dr. Gibson is the author of two books on the historiography of the American Founding, both published by University Press of Kansas. They are *Interpreting the Founding: Guide to the Enduring Debates over the Origins and Foundations of the American Republic;* and *Understanding the Founding: The Crucial Questions.*

David L. Holmes is Walter G. Mason Professor of Religious Studies at the College of William and Mary. He is the author of *A Brief History of Episcopal Church, A Nation Mourns,* and *The Faiths of the Founding Fathers.* Dr. Holmes has also authored numerous articles.

Ralph Ketcham is Professor Emeritus of Citizenship and Public Affairs at the Maxwell School, Syracuse University. Dr. Ketcham has served as a visiting professor to a number of institutions, including Loyola University of New Orleans (2000), Massey University in New Zealand (1998), and the University of Sheffield in England (1996). Dr. Ketcham's works include *Benjamin Franklin* (Great American Thinkers Series, Washington Square Press, 1965), *Framed for Posterity: the Enduring Philosophy of the Constitution* (University Press of Kansas, 1993), and *The Idea of Democracy in the Modern Era* (University Press of Kansas, 2004).

E. Christian Kopff is Associate Director of the Honors Program and Director of the Center for Western Civilization at the University of Colorado, Boulder. An award-winning teacher, Dr. Kopff has been a National Endowment for Humanities Fellow at the American Academy in Rome. Dr. Kopff is editor of a critical edition of the Greek text of *Euripides' Bacchae* (Teubner, 1982) and author of over 100 articles and reviews on scholarly, pedagogical and popular topics. He also authored *The Devil Knows Latin: Why America Needs the Classical Tradition* (ISI Books, 1999), which is widely cited in the new Classical Education movement.

Ralph Lerner is the Benjamin Franklin Professor Emeritus at the University of Chicago, and Professor in the Committee on Social Thought, at the University of Chicago. All of his teaching has been at the University of Chicago, apart from visiting appointments at Stanford, Cornell, and Harvard universities and a visiting lectureship at the Institute Raymond Aron. He has received fellowship awards from the Rockefeller Foundation and the National Humanities Center. Among his publications are: "Commerce and Character: The Anglo-American as New-Model Man," in WMQ, 36 (1979): 3-26 (award winner); *The Thinking Revolutionary: Principle and Practice in the New Republic* (Ithaca, 1987); and *Revolutions Revisited: Two Faces of the Politics of Enlightenment* (Chapel Hill, 1994).

Michael Lienesch is Professor of American Political Thought in the Department of Political Science at the University of North Carolina at Chapel Hill. Dr. Lienesch's writings on early American political theory include *New Order of the Ages* (1988), *Ratifying the Constitution* (1989), and articles and essays on topics ranging from Shays' rebellion to the origins of American conspiracy theory. He has specialized in studying the role of religion in American political thought, and his most recent work is *In the Beginning: Fundamentalism, the Scopes Trial, and the Making of the Antievolution Movement* (2007).

Gordon Lloyd is Professor of Policy in the Graduate School of Public Policy at Pepperdine University in Malibu, California. He has written and lectured extensively on the moral and intellectual foundations of political economy, particularly with respect to the fate of classical liberalism. Dr. Lloyd has edited three books on the American Founding: *The Essential Antifederalist Second Edition: Essential Arguments and Foundation Documents 1176-1791* (Rowman and Littlefield, 2002); *The Essential Bill of Rights: Original Arguments and Documents* (University Press of America, 1998); and *The Essential Antifederalist* (University Press of America, 1985) and is the creator of two teaching American history websites.

Robert D. Loevy is Professor of Political Science at Colorado College, where he has taught since 1968. Specializing in presidency studies and civil rights, he is the author of numerous books, including *Flawed Path to the Presidency, 1992: Unfairness and Inequality in the Presidential Selection Process* (SUNY Press, 1995) and *The Manipulated Path to the White House 1996: Maximizing Advantage in the Presidential Selection Process* (University Press of America, 1998).

Howard L. Lubert is Associate Professor of Political Science at James Madison University where he teaches courses in American political thought and political theory. Dr. Lubert was the recipient of a 2004 National Endowment for the Humanities award for his ongoing study of federalism in the American Founding. He is co-editor of the two-volume anthology *Classics of American Political and Constitutional Thought* (Hackett, 2007) and has published essays on the political thought of James Otis and Thomas Hutchinson (American colonial leaders), John Dickinson, and Benjamin Franklin. His most recent publication is "The New York Constitution: Emerging Principles in American Constitutional Thought," published in *American Constitutionalism in the Fifty States* (University of Missouri Press, 2008).

Pauline Maier is Professor of History at MIT and is the leading scholar of early American history. Her book publications include *From Resistance to Revolution: Colonial Radicals and the Development of American Opposition to Britain, 1765-1776* (1972); *American Scripture: Making the Declaration of Independence* (1996); and a more recent textbook, of which she is one of four authors, *Inventing America* (2002, 2nd ed. 2006). In 1998, she received MIT's Killian Award, given annually to one senior faculty member for outstanding achievement.

Michael W. McConnell is Circuit Judge, U.S. Court of Appeals for the Tenth Circuit. Previously, Judge McConnell was Presidential Professor at the University of Utah College of Law. A former assistant to the solicitor general with the U.S. Department of Justice and a former law clerk to Supreme Court Justice William J. Brennan, he has written extensively about the history of the First Amendment's Religion Clauses and the Fourteenth Amendment. His work has been published in journals such as *Harvard Law Review*, *Fordham Law Review*, and *Virginia Law Review*.

Wilfred M. McClay is Professor of History and holds the SunTrust Bank Chair of Excellence in the Humanities at the University of Tennessee at Chattanooga. His book, *The Masterless: Self and Society in Modern America* (University of North Carolina Press, 1994) won the 1995 Merle Curti Award in Intellectual History, which is awarded by the Organization of American Historians.

Jeffry H. Morrison is Associate Professor of Government at Regent University and a faculty member at the federal government's James Madison Foundation in Washington, D.C. He has also held faculty appointments at Princeton University, the U.S. Air Force Academy, and Georgetown University. He graduated with distinction from Boston College and from Georgetown, where he received his Ph.D. His work has been published or is forthcoming with Johns Hopkins University Press, Columbia University Press, the University of Notre Dame Press, Rowman & Littlefield, and Cambridge University Press. His books include *The Founders on God and Government* (2004), *John Witherspoon and the Founding of the American Republic* (2005), and *The Political Philosophy of George Washington* (forthcoming in 2009).

Walter Nicgorski is a classically trained political theorist whose primary interests are the political thought of Cicero, that of the American Founding, and the theory and practice of moral and liberal education. Dr. Nicgorski's work has appeared in journals such as *Political Theory, Interpretation, The Review of Politics* and the *Political Science Reviewer*. He co-edited and contributed to *An Almost Chosen People: The Moral Aspirations of Americans* (1976) and *Leo Strauss: Political Philosopher and Jewish Thinker* (1994). Dr. Nicgorski has held a Lilly Endowment Faculty Fellowship, as well as research fellowships from the National Endowment for the Humanities, the Bradley Foundation, and the Earhart Foundation.

Marvin Olasky is Provost of The King's College, New York City, and a Senior Fellow at the Acton Institute for the Study of Religion and Liberty. He is the editor-in-chief of *WORLD*, a national weekly news magazine from a biblical perspective. He has written twenty books on history and cultural analysis, including

Compassionate Conservatism, The American Leadership Tradition, The Tragedy of American Compassion, Fighting for Liberty and Virtue, and *Abortion Rights.*

Barbara A. Perry is the Carter Glass Professor of Government and Founding Executive Director of the Center for Civic Renewal and the Virginia Law-Related Education Center at Sweet Briar College. Dr. Perry served as the Senior Fellow for Civics Education at the McConnell Center for 2006-2007. In addition to publishing nearly thirty articles, she has authored eight books, including *Jacqueline Kennedy: First Lady of the New Frontier* (University Press of Kansas, 2004) and *The Priestly Tribe: The Supreme Court's Image in the American Mind* (Praeger, 1999). Her most recent book is *The Michigan Affirmative Action Cases* (University Press of Kansas, 2007).

Saikrishna Prakash is the Herzog Research Professor of Law at the University of San Diego School of Law. A former law clerk at the U.S. Supreme Court, he has published articles on issues concerning executive power and federalism, which have appeared in several law journals including *Yale Law Journal, Virginia Law Review, Columbia Law Review, Chicago Law Review,* and *Texas Law Review.*

Stephen B. Presser is Raoul Berger Professor of Legal History at Northwestern University School of Law. A renowned constitutional law scholar, he has frequently testified before the U.S. House of Representatives. He is the author or co-author of numerous articles and books including, *The Original Misunderstanding: The English, The Americans, and the Dialectic of Federalist Jurisprudence* (1991) and *The American Constitutional Order: Introduction to the History and Nature of American Constitutional Law* (Anderson Publishing, 1999, with Douglas Kmiec).

Ellis Sandoz is Hermann Moyse Jr. Distinguished Professor of Political Science and Director of the Eric Voegelin Institute for American Renaissance Studies. Dr. Sandoz was selected as the Fulbright 40th Anniversary Distinguished American Scholar to represent the United States in Italy in May, 1987. He was appointed by President Ronald Reagan to the National Council on the Humanities and served from 1982-1988. His publications include *Republicanism, Religion and The Soul of America* (University of Missouri Press, 2006); *Political Apocalypse: A Study of Dostoevsky's Grand Inquisitor* (Louisiana State University Press); and *A Government of Laws: Political Theory, Religion and the American Founding* (University of Missouri Press, 2001). He is also the general editor of *The Collected Works of Eric Voegelin* (34 vols., University of Missouri Press).

Colleen A. Sheehan is Associate Professor of Political Science at Villanova University and Director of the Matthew J. Ryan Center for the Study of Free Institutions and the Public Good. Dr. Sheehan also served as Visiting Associate Professor at Princeton University in 2006. Her publications include *James Madison and the Spirit of Republican Self-Government* (Cambridge University Press, 2008, forthcoming);"The Commerce of Ideas and Cultivation of Character in Madison's Republic," in Bradley C. Watson, ed., *Civic Education and Culture*, (ISI Books, 2006); "Madison v. Hamilton: The Battle Over Republicanism and the Role of Public Opinion," *American Political Science Review*, Vol. 98, No. 3, August 2004; and " Madison and the French Enlightenment: The Authority of Public Opinion," *William and Mary Quarterly*, 3rd Series, Vol. LIX, No.4, October 2002.

Garrett Sheldon is John Morton Beaty Professor of Political and Social Sciences and Chair of the Social Sciences Department at the University of Virginia's College at Wise. His publications include *The Political Philosophy of James Madison* (Johns Hopkins U. Press, 2001); *The Political Philosophy of Thomas Jefferson* (Johns Hopkins U. Press, 1991); *The Liberal Republicanism of John Taylor of Carolina* with William Hill (Fairleigh Dickenson University Press, 2008); and *The Encyclopedia of Political Thought* (New York: Facts on File Library of World History, 2002).

David J. Siemers is Assistant Professor of Political Science at the University of Wisconsin–Osh Kosh. Dr. Siemers' research interests include American Political Thought and the U.S. Presidency. He is the author of *Ratifying the Republic: Antifederalists and Federalists in Constitutional Time* (Stanford University Press, 2002).

C. Bradley Thompson is Professor of Political Science at Clemson University and Executive Director of the Clemson Institute for the Study of Capitalism. Dr. Thompson's recent publications include *Anti-Slavery Political Writings, 1833-1860: A Reader* (M.E. Sharpe, 2003), editor; *The Revolutionary Writings of John Adams* (Liberty Fund, 2001), editor; and *John Adams and the Spirit of Liberty* (University Press of Kansas, 1998).

Garry Wills is Professor of History Emeritus at Northwestern University. His many books have won many awards–the Pulitzer Prize among them. He has received nineteen honorary doctorates.

Thomas G. West is Professor of Politics at the University of Dallas. He is also a Director and Senior Fellow of the Claremont Institute. He is the author of *Vindicating the Founders: Race, Sex, Class, and Justice in the Origins of America* (Rowman and Littlefield, 1997).

Christopher Wolfe is Professor of Political Science at Marquette University. Dr. Wolfe's main areas of research are Constitutional Law and Political Theory, and his books include *Judicial Activism: Bulwark of Freedom or Precarious Security?* (Brooks/Cole, 1991); *How to Read the Constitution: Originalism, Constitutional Interpretation, and Judicial Power* (Rowman and Littlefield, 1996); and *Natural Law Liberalism* (Cambridge University Press, 2006). Dr. Wolfe is the Founder and President of the American Public Philosophy Institute (1989), Vice-President of the Thomas International Project, and Co-Director of the Ralph McInerny Center for Thomistic Studies.

Jean Yarbrough is Professor of Government and Gary M. Pendy, Sr. Professor of Social Sciences, with a concentration in political philosophy and American Political Thought. Dr. Yarbrough has twice received fellowships from the National Endowment for the Humanities. Dr. Yarbrough has authored several articles and essays in political thought and public policy. She also serves on the editorial board of *The Review of Politics* and *Polity*. She is currently completing a study of Theodore Roosevelt and a Progressive Critique of the Founders.

Michael P. Zuckert is Nancy Reeves Dreux Professor and Chair of the Department of Political Science at the University of Notre Dame. He has published *Natural Rights and the New Republicanism* and *The Natural Rights Republic: Studies in the Foundation of the American Political Tradition*, which was named an outstanding book for 1997 by *Choice* magazine, as well as many articles on a variety of topics, including George Orwell, Plato's "Apology," Shakespeare, and contemporary liberal theory. His most recent book is *The Truth About Leo Strauss* (2006) with Catherine Zuckert.

ABOUT THE MCCONNELL CENTER
AT THE UNIVERSITY OF LOUISVILLE

The McConnell Center was established in 1991 by U.S. Senator Mitch McConnell and the University of Louisville. McConnell, a 1964 graduate of the University, founded the center based on his belief that "Kentucky's future depends on inspiring talented, motivated leaders."

The McConnell Center is dedicated to providing a non-partisan, well-rounded education that encourages top undergraduates to become valued citizens and future leaders of the Commonwealth and the nation. The Center also facilitates public discussion on the major challenges of our time while encouraging an understanding of our shared past.

McConnell Scholarships for Young Leaders

The McConnell Center is home to one of the most competitive and prestigious scholarship programs in Kentucky. Each year, the Center's scholarship competition attracts outstanding high school seniors from around the Commonwealth. Students apply on-line to the University of Louisville and the McConnell Center, and finalists take part in a two-day interview process. Ten students are then selected as the McConnell Scholars and awarded a four-year scholarship to the University of Louisville.

McConnell Scholars receive tuition scholarships to the University of Louisville, have the chance to meet today's most influential leaders, interact with experts in a variety of fields from across the nation, intern in fields of their choice, and travel the world. In its first fifteen years, the Center has awarded more than one hundred students nearly

$2 million in scholarship money, mentored them to compete for elite national scholarships for graduate school, and helped them travel the world from the Highlands of Scotland to rural villages in China.

Graduates of the program have gone on to further study at such institutions as Harvard Law School, Johns Hopkins University, Oxford University, and Cambridge University in England. Though McConnell Scholars have a diversity of professional interests and academic majors, some students have decided to enter politics and government service and have served in top positions from the Kentucky Governor's Mansion to the White House.

If you are an outstanding young student leader, apply for the McConnell Scholar Program at the University of Louisville during the fall of your senior year of high school. Who can tell where it will take you?

Leadership, Government, and History Institutes for Future Leaders

The McConnell Center annually sponsors weekend seminars and institutes for high school students that feature top experts in fields related to government and leadership.

Professional Development for Teachers

The McConnell Center believes that America's future depends on educating our young people about our history and our political institutions. Realizing that all of us might not be scientists or mathematicians, but we will all be citizens, the Center is dedicated to helping teachers impact the future by teaching our past. The Center regularly runs professional development programs for teachers in a variety of formats, from small seminars to week-long institutes.

Public Education Programs

Every year the McConnell Center hosts educational programs

for the University and general public. The Center's Distinguished Lecture Series has brought more than thirty of today's most important leaders to Louisville, including Secretaries of State Colin Powell, Madeleine Albright, and Condoleezza Rice. The Center also regularly hosts some of today's most interesting authors and experts from a variety of fields. All programs are open to the public and are usually free of charge.

Publications and Scholarship

The McConnell Center believes in the continuing importance of the printed word and the efficacy of first-rate academic scholarship. To enhance our dialogue on perennial topics, as well as the concerns of the moment, the Center has published a variety of pamphlets, small books, and studies on topics from the history of the Senate to the relevance of the Electoral College. Most of these are available in small quantities for educational purposes. The Center also supports the work of a variety of academic leaders doing important research on topics related to American history, politics, and leadership.

Find out more at www.mcconnellcenter.org